A Chester Miscellany:

A Collection of Historical Documents
Gleaned from the Cheshire Sheaf

Featuring the Photographs of

David Heke

Edited by Jon Easton

Fenris Press

Forsan et haec olim memisse iuvabit

Chester . 1999

Printed by Masons Design & Print, Chester 01244 674433

Fenris Press
55 A Garden Lane
Chester, Cheshire CH1 4EW

Published by Fenris Press 1999

A catalogue record for this book
is available from the British Library

ISBN 1-902601-02-5

ACKNOWLEDGEMENTS

Finding a photographer with David Heke's talent living on our doorstep was akin to finding the Sutton Hoo burial in your back garden. When he agreed to work with Fenris on this book, I was confident that his unique vision would ensure that in the text and the photographs we could show this beautiful, historic City in a very different light. These exceptional photographs exceeded my expectations.

The background material for this volume was gathered from a number of sources which require more recognition than the usual bibliography can provide. The principle source for the history of *The Cheshire Sheaf* and the biographical material on Thomas Hughes, F.S.A. was the bound editions of *The Sheaf* (Series 1, Volumes 1-3 and Series 2). The material on *The Courant* was derived from Derek Nuttall's *History of Printing in Chester,* published by the author 1969. I would like to thank Chester Library and Chester City Archives for their assistance in the preparation of this book.

CONTENTS

**Dedicated to the memory of
Thomas Hughes, F.S.A.**

The Old Dee Bridge (above) *The Grosvenor Bridge* (below)

INTRODUCTION

The rationale for Fenris Press has been a mandate to discover and publish historical material which is little known, or difficult to access, along with a commentary to set the material in its context and provide an explanation of its significance. Here we introduce one of our predecessors in the field: the column called *The Cheshire Sheaf* which first appeared on the 1st. of May 1878 in *The Chester Courant*. The contributions made to the *Cheshire Sheaf* will be allowed to speak for themselves, but these remarks will serve to introduce the newspaper, the column and the Editor who was responsible for the first series of the *Sheaf* from which the selections in this book were chosen.

The Courant was the oldest and longest running local weekly newspaper in Chester. It appeared first as the *Adams Weekly Courant* in 1730, becoming the *Weekly Courant* in 1732: its first publishers were the Adams, then the Monk families. In 1832, it was taken over by John Dixon, who moved the presses to Northgate Street and changed its name to *The Chester Courant and Advertiser for North Wales.* (hereafter the *Courant*). In 1851, the *Courant* began to appear in the format which was to be in use throughout the period of the first series of the *Cheshire Sheaf*, (1878-1886). The paper was sold in 1891 and the *Sheaf* re-launched under a new editor.

In the 1880s, the *Chester Courant* was markedly different from what we now expect a local newspaper to be. Before the advent of mass circulation daily newspapers, the local weekly was often the only newspaper most people bought, so it contained not only local news and notices but reports from parliament and the most prominent news from abroad. There were eight pages of text, on paper 18 inches wide by 26 inches long, each page was divided into six vertical columns, although advertisements could run across two columns. There were no banner headlines or photographs and the organisation of the news was different. Top priority on the front page was given to local notices and announcements, followed by Church announcements. The news, which started on page 3, consisted of reports from the city and the local district, 'Welsh Intelligence' and reports from what was then the Imperial Parliament and the foreign news. The columns devoted to the *Cheshire Sheaf* could be found adjacent to the Letters to The Editor, after the local reports but before the news from abroad. It was sold for two old pennies.

Publishing "gleanings historical and antiquarian from many scattered fields" was not an original or unique idea, it was, and indeed still is, a feature of many local and national newspapers. The contents of the *Cheshire Sheaf* were formatted thus;

* Original Documents: A single document or collection of papers of some antiquity usually presented by the editor.
* Notes: Of similar content to the above, but with more 'analysis' and usually material sent in by readers.
* Queries: A forum for readers questions and enquiries, concerning an issue or an entry that had appeared in a previous issue of the column. Occasionally the queries contained a fair amount of information in themselves.
* Replies: Responses to the above.

The variety of material is as large as the field from which it was drawn: that is, the whole history of Cheshire and the surrounding counties. The first issue of the *Sheaf* states that the column "will embrace notes, queries, and replies, stray scraps and quotations, legends, traditions, folk-lore, village customs, local dialect, proverbs, quaint and early literature, personal recollections, old letters and diaries, anecdotes, biographies, archaeology, heraldry, genealogy, parish books and registers, corporate records, architecture and a host of other questions in their specially local aspects". The column appeared weekly until June 1881, "when it came to a sudden stoppage, owing to a severe and dangerous illness of the Editor." Between January 1882 and April 1885 the *Sheaf* appeared fortnightly; after that date it appeared irregularly, ceasing in January 1886.

An example of the workings of the *Cheshire Sheaf* is given here. In the first issue of the column a query appeared concerning a minor matter of Cheshire folklore:

God's Croft The so distant Cheshire prophet Nixon, in one of his occult deliverances, asserts that, when all the tribulations he deals in come upon our land, that there shall be only one safe spot for nervous souls to shelter in, viz., "in God's Croft between the rivers Mersey and Dee." Is there any such field or place existing, within range of the two great rivers referred to in the above quotation?
J. ROGERS

An explanation is necessary, the 'Nixon' mentioned here is the Cheshire prophet who first appeared in pamphlets published at the beginning of the eighteenth century, by the end of the nineteenth century he had become a figure existing on the borderland between history and folklore, and it would appear a well-known one (famous enough nationally to get a mention in Dickens).

Two weeks later two replies were published:

Midway between Frodsham and Helsby there is a farm called "God's Croft." It consists of about 75 acres of flat land, but it cannot be said to occupy any peculiar position. It is in the Frodsham Lordship and township of Netherton, between the Mersey and Delamere Forest.
M. BLEZARD

In your last week's paper an enquiry is made as to 'God's Croft'. Considerable change has taken place in the River Mersey from Eastham-by - Thornton and Frodsham. At some remote period the river and tide must have flowed over Trafford, under Dunham and Helsby. During a storm, the navigation must have been not only uncertain but dangerous. Hence the old designation, now by centuries abbreviated from Hell's Bay to Helsby. Approaching Frodsham is a spot safer for vessels and sheltered; this is called God's Croft. The precise locality is a farm and house formerly occupied by Mr. Arthur Lewis, but now sold to the railway company. This farm-house was one of the earliest homes of Weslyan Methodism in Cheshire; and, far back into the last century, religious services were held there under the wing of the Lewis family.
M. HARRISON

Leaving aside for the moment Mr. Harrison's opinion of the derivation of the place-name of Helsby, the immediate point of interest is the acceptance of the prophetic reference to the extent that it can be given a geographical location as a matter of fact. It clearly interested Mr. Hughes, the Editor, as well. Early in the following month he supplied this contribution to the 'Replies' section:

An interesting article in the Free Village Library recently established by that genuine philanthropist, Mr Joseph Mayer, F.S.A., at Bebington village near Birkenhead, has recently been printed for circulation among friends. The opening paragraph is curiously illustrative of God's Croft and runs as follows:-

"The famous Nixon, sitting on Storeton Hill was asked by his friend, the miller, 'Where a man should find safety on Judgement Day?' The seer replied, 'In God's Croft betwixt Mersey and Dee.' This mystic utterance was long accepted in it's literal meaning, and it gave solace to generations of honest yeomen who dwelt on the promontory upon which the prophet looked. In our day persons trained to the guessing of riddles have ingeniously found another sense to the awful words. By this interpretation they are brought to signify that betwixt mercy and Condemnation - spelt with the initial 'D' after the frank old fashion - sinful man may hope to be saved. This reading is now accepted; so dwellers in this part are deprived of the comforting assurance for the future which their forefathers held.
ED.

This interpretation of Nixon's prophecy was clearly not accepted by everyone, a Mr Donbavand had clearly heard a different story (not, in fact, the 'correct' one as far as the quotation goes), although perhaps his contribution owes more to a desire not to see theology discussed in a newspaper column, and

4

certainly not in connection with the writings of a secular prophet:

I would ask, is not Nixon's indication of a place of safety for men, in the great war he predicted misreported? Did he not answer, or mean, in God's Acre, in the churchyard under the daisies? The story of Nixon sitting on Storeton Hill, discoursing on Judgement Day with a miller, is as apocryphal as his prophecies. Where did the writer of this tract you mention get his facts from?

That seems to have been the end of the discussion on the likely location of 'God's Croft'. What is significant about the material, apart from its value as an illustration of the sort of lively debate the column could produce, is that it is a reflection of the attitudes of the time.

Finally, a few words ought to be said about the man responsible for the first series of the *Cheshire Sheaf,* Thomas Hughes. He was born and brought up in Chester, "an ardent Conservative and Churchman," prominent in Chester public life, he sat on the City Council as a member for St. John's ward from 1868 to 1880 and served as Sheriff of Chester (1873-4). He was influential in the foundation of the Chester Rifle Volunteers, and of the Chester Archaeological Society, in which he served as Secretary from 1856 to 1887. In addition, he belonged to the Royal Archaeological Society, the British Archaeological Association, the Harleian Society, the Record Society of Lancashire and Cheshire and the Historic Society of Lancashire and Cheshire: in 1866, he was chosen a Fellow of the Society of Antiquaries. He published several books on the archaeology of the local area, the most famous of which was *The Vale Royal Of England, or The County Palatine of Chester.* (1852) He was Editor of the *Cheshire Sheaf* from 1878 to 1886.

On April 4th, 1883, Hughes published the following piece describing a like volume to the *Sheaf,* from it Fenris has taken the title for our current volume.

THE CHESTER MISCELLANY

At various intervals correspondents have contributed notices of the Bibliography of Cheshire and its County; and as I have lately had an opportunity of examining a copy of the above work, I have ventured to send a few particulars of it, knowing it to be scarce and difficult to obtain now, 132 years after its publication. The title page runs thus:-

The Chester Miscellany, being a Collection of several Pieces, both In Prose and Verse, which were in the Chester Courant from January, 1745, to May, 1750.
Quidquid agunt homines, concursus, proelia, carmen, Hic epos, hic elegus, nostri est farrago libelli.

Chester. Printed by and for Eliz. Adams; and sold by S. Newton, Bookseller, in Manchester; and M.Cooper, at the Globe, in Pater-noster Row, London
MDCCL

The book is sm: 8vo., and consists of title-page, preface, 2 pp., and 416 pp. of printed matter; 169 of which contain "a series of accounts relating to the Insurrection of the Scots, AD 1745. Their several Marches and Advance, even almost to the centre of this Kingdom; their Retreat and Winter's Warfare in the north, their defeat at the Battle of Culloden and the extinguishment of the Rebellion, by the immediate and other consequences of that Victory." These accounts, so described in the Preface, date from August 22nd, 1745, to the execution of Lord Lovat, which occurred Monday, 8th of April, 1746.

The remaining portion contains a collection of prose and verse consistent with the general taste for essays and elegies. Of those only a few are connected with local history, and cannot claim much notice from your readers; for the subjects are not of an historical or archaeological character, unless the following be considered as such:

"A correspondent, dating ___ in Cheshire, Nov. 20, 1747, says: I doubt not, but most people in this County have heard of a Stone, found some time ago in an adjacent Township, where there was once a great Pool. This Mere Nixon prophesied should come to be mow'n and sow'n, which many years ago, by draining, came to pass. The stone was discovered by the Plough's striking upon it, and was, with no small difficulty, got out of the Earth. I have now, by the assistance of our Exciseman (a University man, but of too much merit to get anything worth while in the Church), put together the letters upon it, and at length made out a legible, inscription of which the following lines are a translation.' "

I have not copied this, which was headed "To Posterity," and consists of thirty-two lines of indifferent verse. Of course I need not remind your readers that the pool mentioned is that of Ridley, in this county but has the stone survived its rescue in 1747 ?

Our University Exciseman, is nameless; I should be glad though to know who this "mutual friend" was that he should be of too much worth for the Church!

There are two elegies on the Death of Sir Watkin Williams Wynn, Bart., which event occurred Sept. 26. 1749, through a fall from his horse when returning from the hunting-field; which accident is referred to as-

"That dreadful stroke, Which gave
The firmest Briton an untimely Grave."

Another poem was occasioned by a visit of the contributor to the spot where this event took place.

"T. W., N-th-p, March 23, 1750," (P T. Wynne, of Northop,) contributes a poem on the Death of Robert Hyde of Nerquis, Esq.; and "Flintensis" sends one, entitled:

"S.M. Thomae Kenyon, filii natu maximi
Lloyd Kenyon de Gredington in Com.
Flint, Armig."

Let us hope that Sir Watkin, Robert Hyde, and Thomas Kenyon deserved the praises our local elegy writers of the last century felt themselves moved to sound!

This is all the local matter that the Miscellany contains, and, although I had expected more it is nevertheless welcome to my collection of Cheshire books. It must be interesting to the present proprietor of the Courant that such a book exists; but more so to feel that The Cheshire Sheaf will be handed down to posterity, as a resource for information (of at least equal interest with The Miscellany) to the local historian, antiquary, and the public at large.

It is probable the Editor of The Miscellany never revealed himself by name; but there was not much lost to us on that score, for there was very little of it that could be safety claimed as original, beyond the local scraps printed in this Note.
JOHN HEWITT

This entry in the *Cheshire Sheaf* illustrates the standard format we have adopted for all the entries. Original documents are set in plain script, Notes, Queries and editorial comments are set in italics. The material has been organised in chronological order by content, rather than the date of its appearance in the column. The list of contents at the head of each chapter contains the date of its publication in the *Sheaf*, the section of the column in which it appeared and the reference number which appears in the bound editions of the column.

What follows is a personal selection, sixty entries out of over two thousand, chosen because they entertained, amused, interested or, in some cases shocked, us. The choice has partly been influenced by considerations of layout and variety - some fascinating longer pieces have been omitted. Some material has been put aside for further and deeper consideration and, it is hoped to bring some of these to press at a later date. The material contained in this volume ranges from an examination of the local legend that king Harold survived the battle of Hastings to die a hermit in Chester, through a detailed description of the fourteenth century City and the actual text of the law that is still frequently and gleefully misquoted in Chester concerning what punishment can be administered to Welsh persons found inside the walls of Chester after dark, to an order governing women who ran public houses in Chester, eighteenth century eye-witness accounts of executions and nineteenth century accounts of hare-coursing through the streets of the city. If there is a single theme to be drawn from the articles presented here, it is that there is often as much to learn about the contributors as from the contributions they have made to the column, special notice should be taken for example of the comments and interpretations often appended to the end of an article. At this point it should also be said that occasionally there are historical inaccuracies and textural errors which have been left uncorrected to produce a faithful copy of the original column. Opinions expressed by the contributors to the *Sheaf* have a certain ring of the nineteenth century about them!

Finally, it is hoped that if you, the reader, have enjoyed or found useful the material below and you happen to be passing Chester Library with an hour or two to spare, you will visit the reference section and find something of interest in *The Cheshire Sheaf.*

The Anchorites Cell

MEDIAEVAL

LIST OF CONTENTS:

MAIDEN CASTLE

Whatever may be the true meaning of this name, I am glad to say that a local tradition is connected with the earthwork on the Bickerton Hills, which, if it does not conclusively prove its derivation to the satisfaction of the philologist, seeks very ingeniously to account for the name.

The inhabitants of the neighbourhood assign no date to the fortress, but say it is very ancient. They further state that once, during war time, the enemy was seen in the distance marching towards the castle; whereupon a number of young maidens threw red cloaks over their dresses, and so placed themselves that at a distance they appeared like an army of soldiers! The enemy, seeing them, imagined that the fortress was well guarded and turned from the attack; and in consequence of this brave act on the part of the damsels, the place has ever since gone by the name of Maiden's or Maiden Castle.
Mill Bank House, Frodsham.
ROBERT HOLLAND

EDDISBURY CAMP

I know of very few places within a radius' of a few miles from our ancient City possessing such interest as Delamere Forest. My object to-day, however, is to speak of its associations in the time of the wars between the Saxons and the Danes. Under Egbert the union of the Saxon heptarchy took place but Cheshire was added to the Mercian monarchy, which became subject to Egbert. Ethelred and his amazon countess Ethelfleda (daughter of King Alfred), restored Caerlleon, called Chester, AD 908 (so says Sir Peter Leycester In his Antiquities) after its destruction by the Danes, and enclosed It with new walls and made it nigh such to as before so that the Castle, that was sometime by the water without the Walls, is now in the town within the Walls.

Ethelred deceased AD 912. His widow Ethelfleda in the year 915 built the town of Eadsbury (or Eddisbury), in the Forest of Cheshire, whereof there nothing remains but that we now call the "Chamber of the Forest", Ethelfleda died at

Tamworth the 12th June, AD 918, and was buried in St. Peter's Church at Gloucester.

Eddisbury Hill lies between Kelsall and Delamere. Old Pale, in this township covers the supposed site of Ethelfleda's City of Eddisbury, and on the summit of the hill are still to be seen extensive earth works, surrounded by a deep ditch, embracing a considerable area of ground. On a recent visit to the spot a friend from the locality, who accompanied me, pointed out one or two mounds, supposed to be the resting place of warriors slain in battle. This hill is considered the highest in the county.

It would be interesting to learn if discoveries have at any time been made, such as old weapons, coins, or anything illustrative of the period when the old city existed ?

Eccleston.

JNO. LEYFIELD

KING HAROLD AT CHESTER

Who will set his wits at work to expound the following quaint bit of History as recorded by the "Monk of Chester"?

"Gyraldus Cambrensis, in his boke called *Itinarius* wolde meane that Harolde had many woundes, and lost his left eye with the stroke of an arrow, and was overcome, and escaped to the countie of Chester, and lyved there holyly, as man troweth, an anker's (anchorites) lyfe, in Saynt James' celle, fast by Saynt John's chyrch, and made a good ende, and was knoweth by his last confessyon and the commune fame accorded in the cytie to that same."

The "commune fame" will surely require some better evidence to support it than the "last confessyon" mentioned above: it being the accepted historical tradition that Harold was slain at Hastings. What supposed evidence have we confirmatory to this statement other than Giraldus?

Glan Aber.

E. G. S.

Though Giraldus was the first authority, so far as we can in these later times prove, for the romantic story about Harold's escape alive from the field of Hastings, and his subsequent hermit-life at Chester; it is not improbable that some such tradition really did obtain credence soon after the battle. The body found upon the field, and believed to be his by his distracted wife and a few followers, was no doubt hastily buried and the impression would then naturally gain ground that identity had not only not been proved, but that their idolised monarch had effected his escape when the fortune of the day turned finally against him.

Chester was at a becoming distance from the field of action, and was moreover known to be a place of strength and security, out of the ordinary travelling track of that day. Hither the popular belief saw the wounded body of their leader secretly conveyed; and the chiefs of his routed army would be well inclined, for state and dynastic reasons, to favour the tradition. Once fairly started, the story would quickly gain consistency in the vulgar mind. This, too, more especially as there was at the time, and so continued for centuries after, a celebrated Hermitage at Chester, on the rock to the southward of St. John's Church, overlooking the River Dee. The hermit himself of that day, perhaps, would not be the one likely to discountenance the tradition, especially as it would add much of outward sanctity and respect to the life he had voluntarily espoused. That the account given by Giraldus was an article of settled faith in his day we may pretty safely conclude; not when afterwards subjected, like many similar traditions, to the light of intelligent criticism, it was found to contain a thousand grains of fiction for one of historic fact. That Harold's royal body lies where accredited history has almost unanimously placed it, there is probably no well-read man of the present day hardy enough to hazard a doubt.

T. HUGHES

Mr. Hughes has put the very best face that could upon the mythical story in relation to the rash but brave Harold, who undoubtedly was killed at the great battle called Hastings.

I have copied out of Mr. William's Ancient and Modern Denbigh, *the following choice bit, relating to the same personage:-*

"In AD 1063, Harold, the son of Earl Godwin, at the head of a formidable army, made himself master of the Vale of Clwyd, and all the level country; and falling suddenly upon Prince Griffith ap Llewelyn, who then held his court at Rhuddlan Castle he took that fortress, and set the Welsh "ships of war" which were lying in the river, on fire, save that in which Griffith escaped "to some foreign land." In the mean time Toston, Tosti, or Tostig, Harold's brother arrived with a strong body of horse, with which to keep possession of the Vale and Rhos, whilst Harold lead the infantry into Snowdonia. The Welsh, unprepared for war, taken by surprise, and without their leader, were forced to submit to the conqueror on his own terms, and to

Godstall Lane

pay tribute. Harold set up monuments of his victories in several places, with this inscription, 'Hic fuit victor Haroldus.' "

Until some better authority is given for this statement, I shall put it down as one of the many curiosities which are converted into history: but here, at all events, we have some landmarks in the "monuments" set up by Harold in divers places with the proud inscription of "Hic fuit victor Haroldus." Now, where are they to be found? I cannot think that Mr. Williams could refer to them so authoritatively if they are not in existence; and I venture to ask him, or some other writer who can do so, to tell us where these "monuments" are to be met with, or the writers who have said they saw them.
A. F. G.

CHESTER STREETS IN TIME OF EDWARD III

Among the first documents entered in the earliest of the Assembly books of the Chester Corporation is one describing the streets and lanes of the city as they existed in the 13th century. This MS. was printed, but so imperfectly, in the first volume of Hemingway's Chester, *pp. 401-4, that I venture to give it verbatim et literatim in* The Sheaf *just as it stands in the original record:-*

Here After foloyeth the names of All the Streetes and Lanes within the Citie of Chester and suburbes of the Same, as the wer named in the dayes of Kinge Edward ye thirdde and afore, by the Recorde thereof in wrytinge, in A table, and copyed herin by the Commandment of the worshipfull Rychard Dutton, Maior of the saide Citie.

In Eastgate Street

On the northe syde of the said strete is a Layne that goithe out of the said strete, By the measeside late William Stanmer, and so into the Kirke yarde of sainte Oswaldes, caulyd Leen Lane. And Beneathe it, upon The same syde, nere the Estgate, is a Layne caulyd sant goddestall Lane, and so goithe out of the Sade strete into the Sade church yarde. This Goddstall lieth Buried within the abbay Churche in Chester, and he was An

Emperoure and a vertuose disposed man in his Lyvynge, and his Lane Lyethe betwene the mease som tymes of Robert Chamb'leyne, and the mease lat in tholdinge of Will'm Humfrey; and uppon the syde nere the estgate ther ys A Lane, caulyd saint Werburge Lane and it Shoutythe into the forsaide church yarde, and over Anendes this Lane on the other Syde ys A Lane caulyd Flesshemongers Lane, And it puttethe upon peper stret.

In Fforgate Strete

Ther is a Lane upon the north Side Sometyme caulled Cooles Lane, and now caulled Cow-lane, and it stetithe into Honwalds Lowe. And nere the Barres upon the South syde ther is A Lane named Love Lane And it putteth upon Bark'rs Lane that goith Estwards into the fildes; and without the barres Ther ys A gayte that goythe downe to the water of Dee, that is namyd Paynes Loode, And upon the other Syde of the Sayde strete more estward is A Lane called Chester Lane, and it puttith upon Honwards Lowe.

In Saint Johan's Strete

In Sant Johns Lane that goithe oute of this strete towards the churche and College, and from it at the cornill of the mansion place of the petite chanon ther is a Lane After the wall of the church yarde, and it is naymed the vicars Lane, and it puttithe upon Barkers Lane and Love Lane; and at the Eynde of this strete Ther goythe a waye downe to the water of Dee, and this Sayde waye is naymyd the Souters Loode."

The Lane in Eastgate street, which Hemingway carelessly printed Peen Lane, unquestionably reads Leen Lane in the original. And an appropriate name it thus bore, for it leaned considerably, running at a sharpe incline by the end of the ancient Buttershops, up from Eastgate street to St. Oswald's churchyard.

Chester Lane, running out of Foregate street, north-westward, was afterwards better known as Horn Lane, an appelation it lost early in the present century.

T. HUGHES

Resuming this medieval record of the Streets of our city as they existed in the days of the third Edward, together with my own meagre notes thereon, I find myself, in company with the ancient scribe,

In Wat'gate Stret

Upon the northe Syde of the said strete next to the churche of Sent Peter is A Lane naymed goslane, and upon the same syde more westerlye next to the mansion place is a Lane named Gerrerds Lane, & it puttythe upon the p'sons Lane; & at the est ende of the trenite churche is a Lane naymed the trenite Lane, and upon the other syde Anendz that Lane is A Lane named Alban Lane, & it putteth upon fosterds Lane.

Berward Stret

Begenneth At the Graye freers gate, and putteth upon Barne Lane; and out of this strete Ther went A Layne to sent Cedde churche, Called sant Chadde Layne, & from the Sayde church ther went a waye to the Waules of the Sade Citie, called Dogge Lane.

Saynt Nicolas Strete.

Begenneth at Watergate strete & putteth upon the nones wall and on the Lane Afore the nones, Callid the nones Lane, which Lane putteth Apon the Castell Lane; and out of this stret goethe a way to the waules of the saide citie, and it is caulyd Arderne Lane, Lying Apon the northe side of the Sade Nunes.

Pepu' Strete

Goith oute of Brugge stret Apon the South syde of the churche of Saynte Michell, & putteth over ffleshemongers Lane to Wolfelde gate in the walles of the Saide Citie, the whych gate some tyme had a Hollo grate wyth a Brugge for . . . . puttyth upon the Souters Loode, and up sent Jones stret & sent John's Lane. This yate was Clossyd up and for donne for so muche as a yonge man in the Somer season toke a mayres Doughter and Bere hair out of pepur strete, as she was playnge at the Baule Amongst other maydens, & yond wyth Hur A Waye. And after, He maryed the same mayde.

In Brige Stret

Uppon the west side is A Lane that is naymd of oulde tyme Normans Lane, and now yt is namyd the comenhall

The Wolfgate

Waye was cauled Shipgate; and Anendz this gate before the Bruge was mayde ther was A fferrye bott that Brought bothe hors and man ou' Dee; & out of the Sayde Cuppynges Lane goithe Bunse Lane, & it putteth Apon the castyll Lane.

In Northgate Strete

Ther is a Lane Afore the gates of the abbey that is cauled the p'sones Lane, and it puttyth upon berward strete; and upon the same side nere the northe gate ys A Lane cauled berne lane, and it puttyth upon berward strete: and out of it goithe A lane towardes the waules, and it ys namyd Oxe lane, and from it towards the northe is caulid bagge lane: and wythout the saide northegat upon the est syde The Lane that ys besydes the lyttell kelne and goyethe northeward towardes the Wyndemyll, That waye ys caulid the Sandye Waye: and without the Sayde northegayte ther is one waye that goythe towardes the Bache and yt ys caulyd the Bache Waye, and ther ys an other Waye That goythe towardes the porte poule, and it ys caulid Poule Waye."

Gerrard's Lane in the above ancient document is now, almost more appropriately, known as Crook Street; for it is still, as we may well conceive Leen Lane in Eastgate Street to have been, a very steep and uneven lane, almost impassable for heavy carts, though sundry improvements have from time to time been made in the gradients. Both these streets must have well earned their suggestive titles in Tudor times.

Alban Lane, now Weaver Street, seems almost to point to some early religious house there dedicated to St. Alban, though I find no trace of such a church in our local story. Berward Street my readers will have no difficulty in identifying with Linenhall Street, a name given to it within the last hundred years. Before that time it was known as Lower Lene (otherwise Lougher Lane), because it was until that period that the west lane on that side of Watergate Street, Linenhall Place and Stanley Street, &c., being then all included within the grounds of the Gray Friars Monastery.

lane, and putteth upon Alban lane, & upon the same syde more Southe is a lane caulyd perpoyntz lane, that was the waye Su'tyme to the com'an haule; & more southerly this Lane ther is an other Lane caulyd ffustards Lane, and we now caule yt the Whyte ffreres Lane, and it putteth upon Sent Nycolas strete, & Beneyth yt upon the Same syde is Cuppyng Lane, and it putteth upon non Lane. And Beneith this saide Cuppings Lane more southerly ys the castyll Lane, and out of it goithe a Lane Towardes saynt marye Church, called sant marye Lane; and nedz the said castyll Lane ends upon the est Syde of the Sayde strete is saint Olas Lane, & benethe it upon the same syde is Clarton Lane, & it puttyth upon the waules of the saide Citie, and Anendz this sade Clarton Lane upon the west ende ther was a waye for horse and man, that went to A gate in the waules of the Said Cittie, the which

13

"Sent Cedde churche" and "Sant Chadde Layne" remind us of another Church not then in existence, nor had it been indeed for at least a century previously. But this is a subject which will deserve separate handling some day in The Sheaf.

Arderne Lane is the present Black Friars Lane, opposite to St. Martin's old brick Church.

The quaint story about the Pepper Gate and the Mayor's abducted daughter is not badly told, though of course amplified and idealised, in Albert Smith's Christopher Tadpole.

Clarton Lane. Hemingway (i. 404) prints this Clayton Lane, but in the original record, which I here print verbatim, it is undoubtedly written Clarton [?for Claverton] Lane.

T. HUGHES

A GROSVENOR CHARGED WITH MURDER

Cheshire Men, when in early times charged with murder or other high crimes or misdemeanours, had at least one chance of saving their necks, if there was any reasonable doubt of their guilt. Their accusers had always to appear face to face with them in court; and if the former's evidence chanced to be shaky, woe-betide them!, for -beyond the prisoners gaining their freedom, their accuser or accusers had to go to gaol in their stead! - yes, and remain there, too, till the following Assize, if not longer.

Thus, in the 34th. year of Edward I (1305-1306) we find it upon record that Warin Le Grosvenor Lord of Budwurth , and a Forester of Delamere a collateral connection (rather far removed) of our Ducal family at Eaton, had brought himself within the stern purview of the law, on a charge of attempted murder! Master Warin, for Ormerod nowhere calls him Knight, was indicted for having shot Sir Richard Pulford with a string and long bow and arrow. The accused, on being brought up to plead, was mute whereupon he was ordered to undergo the punishment of being imprisoned, almost naked, and fed daily on barley, bran, and water, for not pleading guilty, or not guilty, to the serious indictment.

This punishment went on for a considerable time Warin Le Grosvenor's spirit being a crooked one to conquer but hunger unassuaged cannot last for ever, though he probably held out under his peine fort et dure until nature could hold out no longer. So he announced to his gaoler that he was utterly tired and was there and then ready to plead. Brought once more before the Court, and having the indictment read over to him in solemn form Warin claimed that the prosecutor had not given, in his indictment or charge, either the thickness of the fleck (shaft) or the colour of the feather at the end thereof, and that as a consequence the indictment must fail! This was special pleading with a vengeance! but the court took the prisoner's view of the situation, and thereupon decided that the lucky Grosvenor must be discharged; and that Sir Richard Pulford, the prosecutor, for having put a "bad count" into his indictment, must himself go to gaol in Warin's stead! What the result was whether Master Warin was again attached on Sir Richard Pulford's release, and tried for the alleged crime: - or whether their mutual taste of imprisonment had been enough to calm them both down and make them friends, there is nothing in the record to indicate. One thing, however, is certain: - the affair stopped short of actual murder for Warin Le Grosvenor who was son of a bailiff of Over of the same Christian name, did not suffer any great penalty for his supposed misdoing ; for he survived to Edward II (1309-1310), and his children carried down the line of Grosvenor of Budworth until the estates passed through heiresses to strangers.

T. HUGHES

EXPULSION OF THE WELSH OUT OF CHESTER

(Recognisance Rolls, 3 & 4 Henry IV, 1403.)

I copied the other day, at the Record Office, London, the following Royal Writ, addressed by Henry, Prince of Wales (afterwards Henry V) to the Mayor,

Sheriffs and Aldermen of Chester, at a time of the utmost national peril. Shrewsbury had been won and lost only six weeks before, but the pride of Owen Glyndwr had merely been humbled, not subdued: the towns and castles on the Welsh border were in a state of constant alarm, and subject to almost daily attacks from the restless enemy. King Henry, being at that time with his son and the army in Yorkshire, despatched the Prince of Wales south-westward to set our riotous district in order.

Accordingly, he arrived in Chester early in September 1403, and on the 4th of that month issued the following remarkable and very peremptory order to the Mayor and Commonality of the city. It is evident that the loyalty of the Welsh people then in Chester was at least doubted, and probably not altogether without cause, for political or dynastic opinions were in those days rather too evenly balanced to afford any certain guarantee of permanent peace.

"Henry, son of the illustrious King of England and France, Prince of Wales, Duke of Aquitaine, Lancaster and Cornwall, and Earl of Chester, to the Mayor and Sheriffs, and also to the Aldermen of the City of Chester, greeting,

For certain reasons which specially concern the safe custody of our city aforesaid, and accordance with the consent of our Council, we order that forthwith, on sight of these presents, you cause to be driven out without the walls of the city aforesaid all manner of Welshmen of either sex, male as well as female. In such sort that they be thoroughly driven forth of the said city, and that no Welshman, or any person of Welsh extraction or sympathies, or whatever state or condition he may be, remain within the walls of the said city, nor enter into the same before sunrise on any day, on any excuse, nor tarry in the same after sunset, under pain of cutting off of his head; and that on no day whatsoever he journey or presume to go into the said city with arms upon him under pain of forfeiture of said arms except one little knife for carving his dinner. And that they enter into no wine or beer tavern in the same city, and that they hold no meetings or assemblies in the same, and that three of the same Welshmen come not together within the walls aforesaid. Which thing, if they do, they shall be forthwith taken for rebels against the peace, and be committed to our gaol in the city aforesaid, there to remain until we take order about their liberation. And if it happen that any strangers, Welshmen, to wit of our countie of Flynt or other parts whatsoever of our dominions of Wales, shall be plaintiffs at the aforesaid city, then, having left their weapons and harness without the gate by which they are about to enter into the city aforesaid, they shall enter the same unarmed for the doing their business in the same. So that in no wise they pass the night within the walls, under the direst pains. We command that you cause such guard to be ordered, set, and maintained at each gate of the city aforesaid, with watches upon the walls and elsewhere in the same city by night and day; for which guard and watches ye shall be prepared to answer, - and that you cause articles of this brief, referring to the arresting of Welshmen in the city aforesaid and as to their not remaining in the same, to be proclaimed publicly in your bailywick for the informing of the people concerning these ordinances on our part. And you shall carry out this to the utmost of your power, under pain of forfeiture, and be ready to answer should anything happen other than well to our said city.

Given at Chester the 4th day of Spt., in the 4th year of the reign of our said Lord and father King henry the 4th after the conquest.

By The Council.

Rather a warm time this for our friends the Welsh, both men and women! Numbers of them who had seen fit to surrender, and to eat the leek before the conquerors, had been pardoned on certain conditions not over agreeable; but those who remained true to their old colours, were hunted about from place to place without mercy. And as the writ proves, all natives of the Principality, as well as those merely of Welsh blood or sympathies, who had sought homes for themselves in Chester, had to leave the old City at a days notice, on pain of decapitation!

The citizens themselves had taken a somewhat prominent part with Henry Percy, and had joined his ranks in considerable numbers when he passed through the city on the way to the fatal field of Shrewsbury. So they too were in disgrace with the triumphant Henrys: and were only pardoned, two months before the date of the above Writ, on their finding shipping and provisions for the transport of the men going in the royal retinue to the rescue of the castle of Beaumaris.

T. HUGHES

FOOTBALL IN CHESHIRE

I cannot find out when this game was first played in Cheshire: the earliest reference I can trace is in King's Vale Royal. It was during the Mayoralty of Richard Pool, merchant, in the year 1564, and the notice runs as follows: -

"This year there was a great frost, and the Dee was frozen over, so that the people played at football thereon."

J. H.

I know of no very early reference to this outdoor game in our Cheshire annals,- I mean the game as we now understand it, and as ordinarily practised by modern athletes. But I can point to a grim and most scandalous game of Football once played on the old county, which in our own day would have, and very rightly so too, a serious ending for all concerned.

The Abbots and Monks of Vale Royal were at certain periods of their history at terrible loggerheads with their civilian neighbours, who occasionally took odd ways of showing their feelings towards those prominent fathers of the Church. Here is a sample of their occasional amusements.

In the fourteenth of Edward II, 1320, a Commission was issued by the King to Robert Holland, Justice of Chester, to enquire into the death of John de Boddeworth, a servant of the Abbot of Vale Royal; who was stated to have been murdered at Darnhall Abbey by certain brothers from Oulton. I have not seen the original record; but it does not follow that these "brothers" were necessarily monks,- I rather think the reverse. It would seem that poor John Boddeworth (or Budworth) had been zealous, perhaps a little too zealous, in his master's service, and exacting more than was quite agreeable from the amiable folks about Oulton; any way, he was on the day indicated in the record set upon "per fratres de Oldynton", and then and there barbarously killed. Not satisfied with this outrage, his head was cut off by the aforesaid brothers; and thereupon the savage crowd at once commenced a perfectly novel game of Football, using the gory head of the luckless servant as a ball, which they kicked about with great fury and agility. I see nothing in the abstract of the Records as to what was the result of the Commission,- let us hope that the majesty of the law was appropriately vindicated!

G. T.

THE HERMIT NUN OF NORTON

I rejoice to be able, more by luck perhaps than cunning, to offer the following reply to the query of your fair correspondent Lucy D. T., whose contributions to The Sheaf are always "to the manner born."

Were the original chronicle of Norton Priory now in existence and available, I have no doubt we should glean some interesting details about the Hermit Nun referred to in the query. All I can say now is that I have recently found the following particulars relating to the fair recluse in question, who appears from her name to have belonged to a good Cheshire or Lancashire family.

The first known trace of her is in the year 1493, long prior to which we glean that she had been a Nun at Norton Priory and that her name was Agnes Bothe, alias Schepard. In the year named she had by her sanctity or family influence gained the ear of the then Bishop of Lichfield, William Smith, a native of Lancashire; and from him she obtained a licence of removal to a cell near the

Chapel of Pilling, belonging to the Abbey of Cockersand, in that county. I will append a translation of Bishop Smith's licence, which is well worth placing upon available record.

"William, by divine permission Bishop of Coventry and Lichfield, to his beloved brethren in Christ the Lord Abbot of the house of the Blessed Virgin Mary of Cockersand, and to the convent at the same place, brotherly salutation and charity in the name of the Lord. Whereas that holy woman, the Lady Agnes Bothe, alias Shepherd, of the nunnery or priory of the Blessed Virgin Mary of NORTON, inflamed by the zeal of her deeply religious feelings, is very desirous of being separated from the intercourse of men, and especially wishful to be kept from the delights of an enervated age, and to pass a lonely life near the Chapel of Pilling in the parish of Garstang in our diocese, and there to be immured that she may be able to render a careful and devoted servitude to the Most High; and whereas she has indeed for a long time persevered in this happy plan of hers with unchanging vigour of mind, as she still does at this present. We, however, while we approve of this praiseworthy wish of the nun herself and hope that the aforesaid stay there of the Lady Agnes may not only be pleasing to our Most High God, but also have added no small portion to her life who has so deserved it, Therefore we enjoin upon your brotherhood, under the protection of our seal in that regard, that you confine the said Lady Agnes Bothe, otherwise Shepherd, in the house or cell there set apart for that purpose, and to perform, superintend, and carry out all and singular the requirements usual under similar circumstances. whether by law or praiseworthy custom. Given in our manor of Beaudesart, under our seal, Nov. 20, 1493, and in the 2nd year of our consecration."

This document put our lady recluse in full possession of her new anchorite home at Pilling; and eight years afterwards we find from the Rentale de Cockersand, 1501 (Chetham Society, vol. 57, pp. 29-30; vol. 104, p. 105), that she was still alive and there interned. The entry in the Rental runs thus:-

"M'd yat Annes Schep'te hasse payne to James ye Abbott of Cockersand for her lyning, ijs. ijd. to me, & vjs. viiijd. to ye Covent."

Why, remarks that ripe scholar, the late Rev. Canon Raines, this devout nun abandoned NORTON PRIORY for the quiet little cell at Pilling Chapel "will perhaps never be known; but it may be conjectured that it was with the hope of attaining higher degrees of sanctity than she found within her reach amongst the sisterhood of Norton."

G. T.

The Cloisters, Chester Cathedral

CHESHIRE MURDERS, TEMP' RICHARD II

Acts of Parliament in our days are not perhaps the liveliest sort of reading for those not engaged in the profession of the law. But there are many of the earlier

17

statutes, as preserved to us under authority by Berthelet and other early English printers, which would well repay an attentive perusal, and explain many moot points in our national history. I have now before me, for instance, a folio of ten pages, printed in the year 1504 (19th Henry VII), containing the whole of the laws enacted in the first year of Henry IV, he who only just before had deposed his liege lord Richard II at Flint Castle, and conducted him, after a night or two's rest in our Castle of Chester and at Nantwich, as his prisoner to London.

The Acts of this perticular year are mainly those setting aside or altering if not improving those passed by his unfortunate predecessor. The preamble of the session runs thus:-

"Henry by the grace of god, kynge, &c., to the honour of god and the reverence of holy churche, for to nourysshe unytie, peace, and concorde of all parties within the realme of Englande: And for the relief and recovery of the same realme, which now hath been myschevously put to greate ruyne, myschief, and desolacyon; of the assent of the prelates, dukes, erles, barons, And at the instauns and specyall requeste of the comens of the same realme assembled at his parliament holden at Westminster, in the feaste of saynte Feythe the vyrgyn, the fyrste yere of his reygne, hath made, ordained, and stablyshed, certeyne ordeynannces and statutes in fourme as here after followeth.

Cap.1. Fyst that holy churche have and enjoy all his ryghtes, liberties, and franchises, entirely without embleamys-shynge, &c, &c."

Other statutes follow...but it is to Cap. 18 that I wish to draw the attention of the reader; for it refers wholly to our county of Chester, which seems at that time to have stood higher than others in the annals of crime. The act thus proceeds:-

"Item upon the grevous clamour and complaynt made to our sayd soveraigne lorde the kynge in this p'sent p'lyment, of the many murders, ma'slaughters, roberyes, bateries, and other ryottes and offences, whiche before this tyme hath ben done by people of the countie of Chester to dyvers of the kynges liege people in dyverse counties of Englande: The same our soveraigne lorde the kynge, by the advyse and assent of his lordes spirituall and temporall, and of all his comens aforsayd, hath ordayned and stablysshed that if any p'son of the countie of Chestre, resceaunt or dwellynge within the same countie, of what estate or condicyon he be, do com'yt any murdre or felonye in any place out of the sayd cou'tie, p'cesse shal be made agaynste hym by the comon lawe till the Exigende in the counties where such murdre or felonye was done; and yf he flee from them into the countie of Chester, and be outlawed and put in exigende for such murdre or felonye: The same outlawrie or exigende shalbe certified to the officers and mynisters of ye same countie of Chester, and he the same felon taken by the same offycers and mynisters; and his landes and tenementes, goodes and catels, beyinge within the same countie of Chester, seysed as forfayt into the handes of the prynce, or of him that shall be lorde of the same countie of Chester for the tyme, and the kynge shall have the yere and day and the wast. And the other landes and tenementes, goodes and catals, of such felon beynge out of the same countie of Chester, shall remain holly to the kynge, and to the other lordes havynge theof franchyse as forfyt, &c., &c."

It thus appears clear that, as the law stood in the days of Richard II, any Cheshire man committing a felony outside his own county, and finding his way back again within the limits of the Palatinate, was free from arrest and all legal process in the king's name! It is easy to see what iniquities would be possible and indeed certain, under such a system of rival authority ; and we cannot wonder that, bit by bit as centuries rolled by, the crown should assert and in the end maintain its right of legal procedure over the entire soil of England. These rights, it may be added, were only completely established in the present reign, when the distinct courts and jurisdiction of the Cheshire Palatinate were swept away for ever.
T. HUGHES

THE PRINCIPALITY OF CHESTER

Most readers of local history are aware that king Richard II, out of his special regard for his liegemen of Cheshire, and not satisfied to let our county remain a mere Earldom, elected it into a Principality. But few have ever seen, much less read, the Statute under which that dignity was conferred on the Palatinate. We will therefore, from the edition of the Statutes of the Realm printed in 1504 (19 Henry VII) place the ipsissima verba of the Act of 21 Richard II., cap. 9, on permanent and accessible local record:-

"Item our, soveraigne lorde ye Kynge hathe ordayned & stablysshed for the great charyte & affecyon y't he hath in the contie of Chester, & to yo gentyls of the same, & for as muche as the king him selfe before that he dyd take the hye dignitie of kyng, & his honorable father before him, and other his noble p'genitours, have ben Erles of the sayd countie of Chester; and for the great honour of his eldest sonne yf god sende hym any, & of his other heyres whiche shall have ye same seignorye here fter; by the assente & accorde of all the lordes spiritual & temporal, & at the prayer of ye said com'ns,, hath ordayned & stablyshed for him & his heyres, that the sayd countie of Chester shall be the principalyte of Chester, from hensforthe named & holden the principalyte of Chester, with all ye lyberties and fraunchises therof had and used, & in the same maner as it hathe ben before when he was named erle of Chester, for ever.

And more over the kynge of his certayne scyence, & by the assent & accorde aforesayd, & for the ease, concorde, & tranquilyte of his liege people of the sayde principalyte, & of the countyes of Flynt & Shropshyre, & of the seignoryes whiche beloynynge to the same, hathe granted, ordayned & stablyshed that the castoll of Lyons [Holt] with the seignorye of Bromfelde and Yale to the sayde castell belongynge. The castell of Chi'ke with the seignorye of Chirkeslande to the sayde castell belongynge. The castell of Oswaldstrate,

with the towne well walled w't stone, & the hundreds & xi townes to ye sayd castel belo'gyng. The castell of Isabell with the seirnorye to ye Same, belongynge to ye castell of Dallilay with the appurtenannces in the countie of Shropshyre, and the revercyon of the seignorye of Cleve with all theyr appurtenannces whiche Edward erle of Rutlende holdeth for terme of his lyfe: all whiche townes, castels, & seignoryes aforesayd were to Rycharde, late erle of Arundell, and whiche, by force of the judgement gyven agaynst ye sayd erle in the sayd parlyament be forfete to our soveraigne lorde the kynge, shalbe from hensforth annexed unyed and incorporate to the sayde principalyte of Chester, and shall wholy abyde & remayne to the same principalyte as parcell & a nombre of ye same for ever, without beynge gyven, solde, alyened, seured, or departed from the principalyte to any persone by any waye here after.

And that no gyfte nor grav'te at any tyme hereafter be made of the sayde principalyte nor of ye castels, seygnoryes, and townes aforesayde to no person but onely to the kynges eldest sonne whiche shalbe prynce there, yf it please ye kyng to make hym. And that the same eldest sonne which shall have ye sayde pryncypalyte shall have also the sayd castels, signoryes, and townes, as wayed & annexed to the same principalyte withoute beynge severed or departed from the same in tyme to come, so that the sayde rescyauntes and tenauntes of the lands & all the inhabytauntes within the sayde castels, seignoryes, & towns shall have, use, and enjoye, all theyr anncyant lawes, ryghtes & customes there of olde tyme reasonably had & used.

Saved and reserved alwayes to oure soveraigne lorde the kyng his regalye, lybiertie, & fraunchise, and ye ryghtes of his crowne. Provydeprincipalite and the seignoryes aforesayde shall have and enjoye the same lawes, lyberties & customes, usages, eyghtes & fraunchises, of olde tyme in the same reasonably had and used, as playnely and wholly as it was had and used, before the begynnynge of the same parlyament. The name of the countie of Chester changed into the name of the pryncipalyte of Chester, and the annexion and union of the sayde castels, seignaryes, and townes to the same, notwithstandyng."

On the subject of this local Act, the historian Maitland thus writes:

"In 1398, king Richard II. brought into Shrewsbury a numerous guard of the Militia of Cheshire, who expressed so strong an inclination to serve him that, to gratify the county, he erected it into a Principality, and added to the rest of his titles that of Prince of Chester, an appellation however which ceased with its first possessor."

G. T.

GIRL TAVERN KEEPERS AT CHESTER

Unless old Chester has been very much belied by its own medieval chroniclers, the tavern-keepers of the Tudor period were, numbers of them, not the most moral or law-abiding of the citizens. Permissive Bills, Local Option, and Good Templarism were, as cures for this social evil, unknown to these times: but, as will be seen by the following Order of Assembly, the local magistracy of Chester occasionally took the bull by the horns, and did its little best to scotch the serpent of disorder. We find it was set down in the Book of Assembly.

"In the tyme of HENRY GEE, Being mayre of this Citie, the xij day of May in ye xxxij yere of King Henry the eyghte,-

Who shall kepe Ale Howse

Wheras all the tav'nes and alehowses of this Citie have and be used to be kept by yong women, other wyse then is used in any other places of this relme, wherof all straungers resorting hether greatly marvil and thinke it an unconvenyent use, wherby not onely grete Slaunder and dishonest Report of this citie hath and duth run Abrode; in Avoyding wherof, and allso to exchew as well other suche grete occasions & p'vocac'ons of wantonnys, brauels, frays, & other inconvenyentns, as therby doth and may ensu dalye Amongst youthe & Light desposid p'sons, as allso damag's untu ther mast'rs & oun's of the tav'ns and ale houses,

It is ordred by the Said mayre and his Brethern, w't the comon counsell of the said citie, in ye Assimble houlden the daye and yere Above said, that after the xth day of this next monyth of June next coming, there shall no Tavarns nor Alehowsys be kept w'tin the said Citie by eny woman being betwene 14 and 40 yeres of Age, under payne of xls. to be fofyted. By ev'y man or woman That taykyth or Kepyth eny s'n'nts contrary &c."

It will be seen from the date just given that it was exactly 340 years ago this very day that the above stringent Order was passed in the mayoralty of that fierce and earnest Reformer of all local abuses, the sturdy Henry Gee.
EDITOR

WOMAN BURNT AT THE STAKE FOR MURDER

In the 16th century MS. in my collection, is the following entry 1580; -

"In this yeare a woman burned at Boughton for the poysoninge of her husbande."

So far as I have been able to learn, after searching our local annals of crime, there exists no trace, written or printed of the above murder, nor of the execution by burning at Gallows Hill, Chester, other than the meagre entry in my ancient MS. just quoted: but the mere record of the event, so far back as 1589, now that three centuries have elapsed, may not inaptly be placed side by side with that of Mary Heald, who met a like fate in 1763.
T. HUGHES

PLAGUE STONES AT CHESTER

In the 16th and 17th centuries, and even earlier still, when the ravages of the Plague devastated the county once or twice in a generation, trading between the agricultural classes and the district infected almost entirely ceased. Butter, cheese, and the other like necessaries of life were only obtainable with great difficulty, for the county people would not bring their produce into the usual market, or indeed come themselves within spealing distance of those supposed to be at all tainted with the dread disorder.

Accordingly, a sort of suburban market had to be improvised. A stone was set up at an appointed place in the outskirts with cavities made therein, one to recieve the articles sold, and the other which to place the money laid down in payment. Through the last named cavity running water was sometimes introduced, in order to purify the coins deposited from all risk of infection.

I presume these "Plague Stones", as they are called by antiquaries, are not unknown to your Cheshire annals; and I should be glad to learn where any such are now, or have been ever known to be, in existence in the neighbourhood.
CAMBRO-BRITON

The Blue Bell

King Charles Tower

SEVENTEENTH CENTURY

LIST OF CONTENTS:

CHESTER RACE MEETING

The date on which this great Annual Festival was first established on the Roodeye at Chester has often been debated, some authorities contending that no greater antiquity than 150 years ago can be claimed for our local meeting. The following document however, lately met with by me in a volume entitled Grants and Leases, *in the muniment room of the Corporation, is unfortunately undated; but from internal and other evidence, I think it cannot well be later than the year 1612, thus placing the existence of Chester Races in the reign of James the First beyond all question. The interesting record runs literally as follows, and would seem to be especially appropriate for the Race Week number of* The Sheaf.

Articles concerning a Horse Race

"Articles to be performed for Cirtaine orders towchinge the Runninge of a race for twoe bells, and likewise for a Cuppe to be runne for at the Ringe, upon Saint George his day, being the three and twentieth of April, as followeth.

Ffirst, it is agreed upon that the race for the bells, and runninge at the Ringe for the Cuppe, shall be houlden and kepte upon St. George his day, except it fall out to light either upon Saterday or Saboath day, then they shalbe Runne for upon Mondaie next followinge, and the Warninge by the drum' and Cryer shalbe upon Saturday, or the day next before St. George day, not being ye sabaoth.

The Bell.- Secondlie, every man that bringeth in his horse for the race shall put in to Runn for the bells, 20s., Except him that bringeth in the best bell, Which shall pay but 6s. 8d., and him that bringeth in the second bell, 13s. 4d. And he that winneth the best bell shall have twoe partes of the money that is laid downe. And he that winneth the seconde bell shall have the thirde parte, which is the Residue of the money that is putt in. And every one that rydeth shall Waye, be made in weight, just tenne stone Waight. And to be wayed upon the Roodey in a paire of Scales, which shall be set upp neare unto the house where the Maior and his bretheren standeth.

The Ringe. Thirdlie, everie one that runneth at the ringe for the Cuppe shall put in 2s. 6s. a man, excepte him that bringeth in the Cuppe according to his Covenante by bound at the tyme appointed, whoe shall put nuthinge in for three tymes Runninge at the ringe. And whosoever doth take it the first three tymes shall have the use of the Cupp, accordinge to the Covenantes, and soe much Money as was put in. And if none doe take it the first three tymes, they shall all loose their money that they put in at the first; and the said money to be given to the Maior for the tyme beinge for the use of the poore and prisonners of the Northgate. And they all, or as many of them as please to put in newe money, viz. 2s. 6d. everie man, as before is menco'ed, to have all the last Money that was putt in, and the use of the Cupp as afore is expressed. Provided allwayes, that he that shall Winne the game shall pay and give to the prisonners of the Northgate, vs and to the Clarke for Writing of their names downe, ijs. vjd.

Fourthlie, they that Winne the bells shall give to the prisonners in the Northgate, 10s., viz., he that winneth the best bell shall give 6s. 8d., and he that winneth the seconds, 2s. 4d. if they runne above three horses. And if they Runne but three, they shall alowe but vjs. viijd. onelie to be paid equallie amongest them.

Fiftlie, he that Winneth the Said belle and Cuppe shalbe bounden to the Maior and Citizens of the Citie to bringe in the said belle and Cupp every yeare, with one or twoe sufficient sureties for the delive'y of the said belle (of the same Waight and goodnes as they Were When they Receaved them) upp to the Maior or his deputie for the time beinge, upon St. George his day, in the Inner Pentice of the said Citie of Chester, before twelve of the Clocke at Noone upon the same day, beinge the three and twentieth of Aprill, upon payne of forfeicture of theire boundes. Allsoe they shall pay to the Clarke, when they doe enter into bounde, for makinge theire boundes, 12d. for every boundc.

Lastlie, for givinge of the starte,

either Mr. Sheriffes for the time beinge, or Whome Mr. Maior will appointe. And that noe horses, geldinges, or Mares shall come upon the Roodey, but onlie those that doe runne, untill the Race be ended. And allsoe that the ryders shall not offer one to another any foule play in their ridings, upon payne of imprisonment. And these Articles and orders to be kept and performed unviolated. upon payne of punishment and forfeicture of their bounds and Covenants, as before is sett downe."

It is clearly enough seen from these Articles, that the Chester Race Bells and Cups were what would be termed in the present day 'Challenge' Cups and Bells, held by the winners for one whole year; they contracting under bond for their safe return to the Mayor and Sheriffs, in time for the Races on the following St. George's Day.
T. HUGHES

CHESHIRE FOLK LORE: CATTLE BLESSING

From days far beyond record it was a common custom in Cheshire to use incantations for the prevention of disease and other evils happening to Cattle and for the cure of those beasts which their owners or those who were near neighbours to them, believed to be actually languishing under some Satanic spell. The older collectors of wild plants and other simples, in the hedgesides and on the mountain tops, accustomed themselves to the rude study of these roots and their flowers by means of the household crucible they extracted the virtues they had learnt to regard as peculiar to their use, applying them in salves and potions to the cure of diseases, whether such occurred in their own families or among their cattle. By degrees, as they succeeded or failed in their semi-medical practice, they would come to be set down by their neighbours either as wise and cunning women, or as bad, mainly because unlucky, Witches! Give a dog a bad name, &c., was never more true than in the case of these often very innocent creatures, male or female, who fell under judicial or the popular anger.

I have been led, more or less, to this line of thought from the reading of an ancient tome sent forth in 1617 by a Cheshire Parson, one Thomas Cooper (otherwise Cowper), who had been a Select Preacher at Chester at the very beginning of the 17th century. Having been promoted thence, in 1601, to the Vicarage of Great Budworth, Master Cooper must have made that parish pretty hot for all who came within the scope of his Mystery of Witchcraft *which he published, in small 12tvo., in 1617, and dedicated to the Mayor and Corporation of Chester whose servant he had for several years previous thereto been. At p. 71 he writes, when describing the proofs of the Witches' league with Satan:-*

"A third marke of this secret Covenante is an ordinarie taking of God's name in vaine; specially in blessing of Cattell, which, although the ignerant and unbelieving world hath taken up of custome, yet the first tutors hereunto have beene the Witches, thereby to colour their sorceries, and draw more Proselites to their devotion. . . .such goe to Blessers, to scratch, to use spells, &c., to helpe and do goode, and these are called Good Witches, Wise and Cunning Women . . . Yea, certainely, the Bad Witch, by hurting, makes way for the Good witches helpe and so thereby encreaseth her sinne; or the Blesser, in helping, bewrayes the Bad Witch, and, so many times, brings her to the Gallowes."

Again at p. 211 - "As the Badde Witch hath onelie power to hurt, so the Good Witch or Blesser hath onelie facultie to do good, to helpe, &c., and that in a league with the divell: by which it appeareth now plainely, That the blesser or good witch (as we terme her) is farre more dangerous then the Badde or hurting Witch, &c., yet while the badde Witch usually is haled to punishment, the Blesser is spared, and so permitted to doe more mischiefe, &c."

And so at our Cheshire as well as at Lancaster Assizes numbers of these half ignorant creatures were, under "our sapient monarch's rule," done to death in the name of law and religion Bad as some people will have it we are in this nineteenth century, we have at all events improved, and not a little either, on that ignorance and superstition of which Master Cooper, the puritan parson of Chester and, later on, of Great Budworth, was so sturdy a patron!
Y. O. M.

A TRAGEDY AT THORNTON, NEAR CHESTER IN 1634
'SUMMER ALES'

In a very scarce pamphlet entitled A Divine Tragedie lately acted, or A Collection of sundrie memorable examples of God's judgements upon Sabbath-breakers and other like Libertines in their unlawfull Sports, happening within the Realme of England; in the compasse onely of two years last past, since the Book *[i.e. The Book of Sports] was published by that worthy Divine, Mr. Henry Burton, is the following Note relating to Cheshire.*

"1634. At Thornton, near Westchester the people there, upon the first Publishing of this book, prepared for a solemn ' summer-ale'. The bringing in of their Lady Flora should have been guarded with a marshall troop: the lustiest wench and stoutest young man in the town were chosen to be the purveyors for cakes, and for ribbons for favours. The solemnity was to be on the Munday, but the preparation on the Lord's Day. This lusty, tall maid, on the Satarday before, went to the mill to fetch home the meal for cakes on her head, she being strong and able for the purpose but in the way, passing by a hedge, she was suddenly struck by a divine stroke, and fell into the ditch, where she was found dead. She was suffered to lie abroad in that pickle all the Lord's day till Monday morning, when, the Coroner being Sent for, she was thence carried to her grave immediately; where all her solemnity was buried with her, and all her vain thoughts, in that verie day wherein the great solemnity should have been. And see what a good effect this wrongt in the whole town! First, all their mirth was turned into mourning, no 'summer ale' kept, and besides that, they being moved by the dreadfull stroke of God took their May-pole down, which they had before set up; and never after would presume to set it up again, or to have any more Summer-ales, or May-games. God grant they continue in their sober mindes, and that all other would learn to be wise by their example!"

The above account gives an interesting illustration of the manners and customs in vogue in Cheshire in the early part of the seventeenth century. The "Summer ale" would probably be on Midsummer day.

Pensarn, Abergele
J. P. EARWAKER

THE PLAGUE AT CHESTER, 1647

Of this particular visitation of sickness, out of the many that at various periods have devastated Chester, our local annals give us but a slight description. In Broster's History of the Siege of Chester, even the year of its occurrence is mis-stated; although he tells us that more than two thousand of the citizens died of the dread distemper, and that business so completely ceased that grass grew in the principal streets.

Midsummer, 1648, is the date given by Broster; but when we find, as we presently shall, that it occurred a year previously, we shall see at once that less than five months had elapsed since the city emerged from the horrors of civil war, and from a most violent and protracted siege. This then was the legacy left to old Chester on the close of that gallant and loyal struggle. Pestilence carried off by thousands those whom the sword had failed to reach.

The Plague prevailed beyond the

Whitefriars Street

26

citizens' power to cope with it; and parliament was constrained to put forth its hand to help. Accordingly an Ordinance was passed in the following terms:-

"Whereas Chester is grievously visited with the pestilence, very few families being clear by reason whereof almost all persons of ability have left the said city, there remaining for the most part only the poor, who are altogether deprived of trading, and if not presently relieved are likely to perish for want, and endanger the infecting the adjacent counties.

And whereas the County of Chester is exeedingly impoverished by the late war; 'tis ordered that the ministers of London and Westminster, these in the Counties of Chester, Kent, Sussex, Surrey, Essex, Southampton, Middlesex, Hereford, Cambridge, Suffolk, and Norfolk, do, on the next Lord's Day after the receipt of this ordinance, earnestly move their people to contribute for the relief of the said distressed inhabitants."

These writs or briefs went forth to the churches the several counties named but the aggregate money results, if recorded, have never met our eyes. We are indebted, however, to the research and great kindness of Mr. Charles Bridger, of South Kensington, for three documents from the Public Records, throwing some curious light upon this sad epoch in Chester history. The first document runs as follows:-

Letter from Thomas Atkin, Ex. Lord Mayor of London, to the Mayor and Corporation of Norwich, urging subscriptions for the relief of the inhabitants of Chester.
Laus Deo. London, the 19th Aug., 1647.

"Right worship'll, my due respect remembred unto yow and all your Bretheren. S'r, there was lately an ordinance passed both howses for a collecton for the Citty of Chester and some places there nere unto, being most greviously visited with the plauge (sic), after so long sufferings by the Soldery in those partes the collection is to he made in many counties, but Norwich and some other places are not named, not doubting but such corporations are senceable of

each others sufferinges. I am requested by the Maior of Chester, being here in the howse, and by his ffellow Burgesse, to move yow on theire behalfe that yow would be pleased, either in your Churches or your Wards, to further such theire desiers and so not doubting of your assistance, in so good and charitable a worke, I take leave and rest your worshipp' to command
THO. ATKIN.
To the Right Worshipp'll
John Utting, Esquire,
Maior of the Citty
of Norwich,
in Norwich."
EDITOR

In appropriate sequence to the article on this subject in The Sheaf for October 1st (thanks again to our good friend Mr. Charles Bridger, of London), we print the following letter. It was addressed by Thomas Wodehouse, and Miles Corbett the Regicide, to the Mayor of Norwich, soliciting subscriptions and collections in aid of the stricken City of Chester:

"Westminster, 2 Sept., 1647.
Gentlemen,

The sadd condic'on of ye Cittie of Chester; having lately tasted of ye sword, and nowe lies under ye Plague -being presented to us by p'sons of trust and integritie, We held it our dutie at theire Request to present the same to you, desiring you to imploye your interest and power, that the Ordinance of Parliament, and necessities of the place, may be presented to the people. And we doubt not but the Charitie of such whose hearts God shall incline therein, wil be imployed by ye p'sons menc'oned in ye Ordinance to the uses therein declared, All which we leave to yo'r Christian considerac'on,
Resting
yo'r assured friends to serve you,
THO. WODEHOWSE.
MILES CORBETT

To the Right Wor'll John Uttinge, esqr., Major of the Citty of Norwich, these.
Norwich"

What amount was raised altogether, in the several districts appealed to, for the good citizens of Chester in this dark hour of trial, we know not. The following list, however, fortunately preserved with the series of letters we have now printed, will show what the men of Norwich did towards meeting the distant emergency :-

Collection for the infected poore of The Citty of Chester. *(Here follows a list of donations and their sources.)*
EDITOR

GOD'S PROVIDENCE HOUSE, CHESTER

There is no house in the city of Chester that excites the attention of strangers and tourists more than the old one in Watergate Street, which contains on the beam, supporting the front portion of the house above the Row, the inscribed line: "God's Providence Is Mine Inheritance."

This house was restored, rebuilt indeed, for its then and still owner, Alderman Robert Gregg, about 21 years ago. The late Mr. James Harrison was the architect employed who in the most praiseworthy manner retained all its original features, even to, I believe, the beam containing the inscription. Originally, the date 1652 was to be seen on the beam above what would be reckoned, from the street, as the second-floor window.

The motto, according to Hemingway (History of Chester, *vol. ii, p.5), was "said to have been inscribed by the occupier, as a grateful memorial, after escaping the Plague which had visited almost every other dwelling." but the only record of any devastating Plague that occurred about that period was the one that appeared in 1647 (Cheshire Sheaf, vol. i., pp. 279, 306, 569), five years before the date on the beam. As this is, all the information I have been able to glean from any of the local histories, I have ventured to make the following remarks, with the hope that some of your correspondents may throw some further light on the subject.*

Richard Boyle was created Earl of Corke in 1620 "the great Earl", as he was called, and it was in consideration of such a series of successes as his life was attended with, that he chose that motto - "God's Providence is my inheritance," and which the family still retain (vide a Letter from the Rev. Joseph Boyse, dated 1695, in Thoresby's Correspondence, vol. i., p. 265). His wife Lady Cork, died in 1629, and was buried in St. Patrick's Cathedral, Dublin, and on her monument was inscribed "God's Providence is our inheritance." The line was therefore adopted by one of the leading men of the day, thirty-two years before it appeared on the house in Watergate Street.*

The practice of inscribing sentences., often of a religious character, over external doorways windows, &c., and even on inner walls, was common in the 16th and 17th centuries in England, as well as on the Continent generally. We have no record as to whether the Earl of Cork originated the sentence, or whether he adopted it from some other source. That this latter is by no means improbable would appear from the following passage in Collinson's Somersetshire *(vol. ii., p. 31):-" Over the door of three ales-houses at Mine-head, Somersetshire, is an inscription stating that 'Robert Quirck built this house Anno 1630, &c., and terminating thus.'-*

*"God's, Providence
Is my Inheritance, R. Q."*

This was only ten years after the Earl had been raised to the peerage. He, however, according to Thoresby 's Diary *(vol. 1, p. 429) " used to inscribe in the palaces he built," the same motto so that R. Q may after all have copied from the Earl. Its introduction into Chester, it is evident, did not take place until long after its employment elsewhere, and at a time when it must have been well known; it is therefore fair to infer that the occupier of the Watergate Street house was not the author of the motto, but that he had copied it. Could it be proved he had been in the Earl's service, this would have accounted for it. That he inscribed it as a memorial of preservation from the Plague appears to me to be open to grave doubt. It seems to me more probable that ho only followed a* prevailing custom of the period in which he lived.

In Batenham's etching of the house, executed in 1816., the figures of three upright anchors appear in the space between the window and the inscribed beam. These had been removed, if I remember right, long before the alterations, that took place1861. Were they the arms of any local family?
Budleigh Salterton, Devon
T.N.BRUSHFIELD, M.D.

P.S. In the Antiquarian Chronicle, puhlished by Fennell, there is in the first number, published in June last, a list of mottoes, from Posy Rings at p. 13, and amongst them is the following with the date:
"God's Providence is our Inheritance."
1711.
T. N. B.

WITCHES HUNG AT CHESTER

At page 32 of Broster's Cheshire Biography, 18mo., 1876, there is a note at foot of the page remarking that in searching the parish registers of St. Mary's Chester, he found this curious entry:-

"Three witches hanged at Michaelmas, and buried in the corner of the churchyard by the Castle ditch, 8th October 1656."
Great Saughall
W. H. B.

LADY CALVELEY'S SEAT IN
ST. OSWALD'S CHURCH

It is not often that the title to a seat in a parish church can be proved by incontrovertible evidence to legally vest in the descendants of a single house or domain for two centuries at least prior to this current one. But that such cases do here and there exist and that in our own County and city, too,I am enabled to establish through the courtesy of S. H. Sandbach, Esq., of Broxton Old Hall, the present owner of Lea Hall, near Aldford, but in the parish of St. Oswald's, Chester.

The ancient Chapel of Bruera (otherwise Church on Heath) belonged to the Abbey of St. Werburgh from the period of the Conquest and the owners and tenants of the lands adjacent had been accustomed to baptise, marry and bury in the Cemetery at Bruera, though apparently entitled from a still earlier date to the rights of sepulture at their mother church of St. Oswald's. It must be remembered that in Norman times there was no church save St. John's nearer to Bruera on its south-eastern side, than the interlapping Chapel of Boughton (which was. also part of St. Oswald's), and the Hospital of St. Giles' (otherwise the Spital), which latter chapels adjoined each other on the east side of the city. At the Reformation, Bruera Chapel was served at intervals by the Vicar of St. Oswald's, the Dean and Chapter of Chester of right presenting thereto. The Calveleys of Lea, with their tenants, owned and occupied the chief sitting accommodation there; but as time wore on, and as fashions altered likewise, they changed their residence for a great part of each year to Chester, and their place of worship to the parish church of St. Oswald. The Calveleys were honoured residents within this city parish, and the highest seats in the synagogue were allotted to them; for they were munificent benefactors to that parish church, as indeed they had often been to the Cathedral itself aforetime. There is an official document in the "Chancellor's Court," and copied into a thin folio MS. book, once the Rentail and particular Survey of ye manner of Harthill, of all Mr. Hugh Calveley his lands there, &c.; which MS. Volume has come into the hands of Mr. Sandbach as reigning owner of "The Demeane of Lea." The Document runs in the following terms:-

"John Wainewright, Doctor of lawes, one of the Com'rs of the most Reverend Father in God, Accepted, by Divine Providence Lord ArchB'p of Yorke, Primate of England and Metropolitaine to whom all Jurisdiction Sp'uall and Ecelesi'all within the Dioces of Chester, during his Graces Metropoliticall Visitac'on, now depending, doth belong and Appertaine, To All Christian People to whom these pr'sents shall come, greeting:-

Whereas the Virtuous Lady, Dame Mary Calveley, widdow, a constant and Good Church-woman and frequenter of Divine Service, especially at the Cathedral, where her charity hath been eminently extended, Is now an Inhabitant within the City of Chester, and hath a good and Considerable Estate, lying within ye Parish of St. Oswalds of the same City, for which she pays a considerable proportion of all Leyes and Duties; And in which Church she hath no Constant seat or Pew to sitt in; We, therefore, taking these things into consideration; As also that there is a Pew or Stall, the next save One towards the East from that where the Maior of the City for the time being, com'only used to sitt, haveing the North End thereof adjoining to the Middle isle, In and to which stall or Pew, it doth not appear, that any one hath or maketh any Claime or Title, Doe, as much as by Law we can, grant, assigne Allot and Confirme the aforesaid Pew or Stall into this said Dame Mary Calveley, to Sit, Stand, Kneel, and hear Divine Service and Sermon in, and upon Sundays and Holydayes and at other Times of Publique Worship, for her self only, and whom else she pleaseth to Admitt there for performances of the Duties afores'd.

In Testimony whereof we have hereunto putt the Seals of our Office, the Third of ffebruary, in the Year of our Lord 1662."

There are other Documents, &c., in his curious old Volume of Accounts, that relate in the main to the question of this "pew or Stall,"-which was made a subject of litigation in the Ecclesiastical Courts at Chester for a period of some fifty years. To several of these records, so interesting from a local point of view, I shall in following issues of The Cheshire Sheaf *have the pleasure prominently to allude.*
T. HUGHES

After the Restoration, and indeed before, during the Interregnum, there were several passages of arms between the Calveley family and the vicar of St. Oswald's, nominally, but really the Dean

and Chapter of Chester, as to the Pew or Stall allotted to her by the 1662 decree of Chancellor or Commissioner Wainright. Upon her ladyship's decease, Sir Robert Cotton, heir to the late Sir Hugh Calveley through his mother, took up the cudgels to maintain his rights to the Pew in question, as we may read more at large by perusing the following synopsis of Sir Robert Cotton's Case,

"1615 By a Mapp or Card describing the Seats in St Oswalds Church, Sir Hugh Calveley's ffamily is menc'oned to have a good Seat near ye Pulpit, end next to S'r George Booth's seat.

1649 By a second Map, the Lady Calveley's Seat is taken notice of; but the Church having been Uniform'd, the Seat is in another place, but was built on a Void piece of Ground, at the Sole Costs of the Lady Calveley, and Constantly Repaired at her Costs.

1662 13th February. By a ffaculty; the said last menc'oned Seat, being ye Pew next save one Towards the last having the North End adjoyning to the Middle Isle; Was Graunted the Lady Calveley, by John Wainright Doctor of Lawe, one of the Com'rs of the Arch-B'p of York. Vide a copy of the ffaculty ante.

1677 The same Entrys in a Third Map.

1704 The same Entrys in a fourth Map.

Note:- There are six Gentlemen's family's that Claime Seats in the s'd Church by pr'scription, vizt,
John Massey, Eq'r., W'm. Gamul, Esq'r., John Hurlestun, Esq'r., John Spencer, Esq'r., and Mr. Hulton. The Dean and Chapter alledge all ground in the Church is theirs.
T. HUGHES

THE MAYOR OF CHESTER'S PILLORY
This engine of punishment formerly occupied the angle of Junction of the Bridge street and Eastgate street Rows, opposite the High Cross and the Pentice. Your correspondent, G. T., states it to have faced the latter; but this appears open to some doubt, as an Old Cestrian,

who witnessed the last employment of it, informed me its occupant had his face turned towards Bridge street. Its position is mentioned at some length in the Act of Parliament of 2nd of George 3rd (1761-2). It was apparently (together with its companions the Whipping Post and Stocks) a fixture, and employed only for the punishment of City offenders. There was, however, another Pillory within the City boundary, situated at the top of Castle-street, and used for the punishment of offences committed in the County proper. The first-named was, therefore, par excellence 'the Mayor of Chester's Pillory.'

Some years since I endeavoured to trace back the history of this particular Pillory, but could find no early or even mediaeval allusion to it. There is but little doubt it was used as a City punishment from a very early period. It was well known and practised by the Saxons as the Halsfang, and under the Norman feudal system was one of the essential appendages to the View of Frankpledge

The earliest authenticated instance of its use in Chester that I have met with is thus detailed in No. 1929 of the Harleian MSS:

"On Aug. 13, 1663, at Chester, one Fox of Ireland was arraigned for speaking treason, viz., that as he had lately prosecuted the late King to death, so he would do this. On Saturday after, he was adjudged to the Pillory, where he stood ... hours and lost his ears"

The next mention appeared in the News of Aug. 18, of the following year:

"Chester, Aug. 15. Upon Monday last here was tried One Pool (formerly a Sequestrator) for Seditious words, which being proved against him, he was adjudg'd to stand in the Pillory two hours at the time of Market, and & fin'd hundred pounds to his Majesty."

In Randle Holme's Academy of Armory published in 1688, is the representation of a double Pillory, and it probably depicted the City engine of punishment of that date. Offenders when placed in it were, according to his description :

"to be mocked, derided, and made a common spectacle, that all Beholders may see and beware of the like offences, and do no such wickedness."

The Corporation accounts make but little mention of it, the earliest I have found are the following:

1747 Paid the guards for attending Bithell in the pillory: 6s 0

1771 April 27 Paid twelve constables by Mr. Mayor's order for attending whilst Mary Axson stood in the pillory: 12s 0.

The last occasion of its employment was during the Race week in the year 1800, when a bricklayer named Steele was exhibited in it. My informant, who was an eye-witness of it, told me Steele was very severely pelted by the mob, and it reminded him of the following passage in Gay's Trivia (book 2),

"Where elevated o'er the gaping crow.
Clasped in the board the perjur'd head is bow'd,
Betimes retreat; here, thick as hail-stones pour,
Turnips and half-hatch'd eggs, (a mingled show'r)
Among the rabble rain,- some random throw
May with the trickling yolk thy cheek o'erflow."

Very shortly afterwards, and probably in consequence of the severe treatment resolved by the occupant, the City authorities directed the removal of the Pillory and the necessary abolishment of this form of punishment. The order for this appeared in the Assembly Book of the Chester Corporation in the following words:-

"At the Assembly held in the Common Hall on May 26, 1800. Ordered, on the recommendation of the City lands Committee, that the Pillory and Stocks at the Cross shall be pulled down as soon as convenient, in order to improve the turn at the end of Bridge Street, under the directions of the City Treasurers, who are to be supported by this corporation, in case any action or actions shall brought against them."

One of the first Acts of the first Parliament (1837) held under her present

Majesty was to abolish the use of the Pillory, which then happily passed into the list of Obsolete Punishments. Let it be recorded to the honour of the Chester Corporation, that they had the courage and humanity direct its abolition in their City, 37 years before.

Brookwood Mount, Surrey.

T. N. BRUSHFIELD, MD

THE ORDER OF THE ROYAL OAK

After the restoration of monarchy in the person of Charles the second it was proposed to institute a new order of knighthood, the members of which were to be styled the "Knights of the Royal Oak", in honour of the then popular "Twenty-ninth of May." Only those were to be considered eligible for the distinction who had rendered special and important service to the "Martyr King," and had distinguished themselves in the late troubles. The project was however abandoned, it being judged that the institution of such an Order "might create heats and animosities and open those wounds afresh which at that time were thought prudent should be healed."

In the MS. of Peter le Neve, Norroy, a list of the intended Knights is given, Cheshire furnishing a very considerable contingent, as will be seen by the following names which appear among the number:-

	Value per an. £
Darcie Savage	1,000
James Poole, Esq.	2,000
Thos, Cholmondeley, Esq.	2,000
—— Legh, of Lyme	4,000
Sir Thos. Wilbraham Kt. (Woodhey)	3,000
John Crew, Esq.	1,000
Edw. Spencer, Esq.	600
Henry Harpur	600
Roger Wilbraham	1,000
Roger Grosvenor of Eaton	3,000
Sir Thos. Mainwaringe Kt.	1,000

It is worthy of note that one of the proposed Knights was Mr. Henry Cromwell, "first cousin, one remove to Oliver, Lord Protector," a zealous royalist who had been instrumental in the restoration of the King; but who, knowing that "the name of Cromwell would not be very grateful in the court of Charles the Second, disused it, and styled himself only plain Henry Williams, Esq., by which name he was set down in the list of persons as were to be made Knights of the Royal Oak."

Upton Macclesfield

JAMES CROSTON

ST. THOMAS COURT, CHESTER

For centuries prior to the Reformation the Abbots of St. Werburgh, and since that time the Dean and Chapter, regularly kept their half-yearly Court for their Manor of St. Thomas, in the ancient refectory of the Abbey. The Chapter only discontinued the custom some 80 years ago. The Cathedral tenants were the jurors, and the Chapter Clerk usually acted as seneschal of the courts.

As an example of the work done on those occasions, the following, taken from the records of this court, held October 25 1693, will not be without local interest.

"St. Thomas'. View of Frankpledge "cum curia," of the Dean and Chapter of the Cathedral Church of Christ and blessed Mary the Virgin, held for the manor aforesaid, on Wednesday, to wit, the 25th day of October, 1693 before Robert Ffoulkes, gent., seneschal there.

Wee the Grand Jury, &c., doe present at the Court now held, as followeth,-

We p'sent all those that owe suit and service to this Court, and have not appeared this day, haveing had Lawfull warning, and amerce them in twelve pence a peece

We present Mrs. Swift, widdow, for not keeping the Abbey Court Well in repair, and do amerce her in the sum of ten shillings.

We present Will. Nicoe for not rebuilding the wall between him and Thomas Lloyd [in God's-stall Lane], and do Amercie him in thirty shillings.

We present the Townshipp of Trafford for not repairing the Moore-lane

Cawsey, and doe Amercie it in the sum of three shillings foure pence betwixt and May next.

And also for not repairing a Platt leading to the Hall, and doe amercie it in the sum of 12d. by the same time.

We present Richard Cartwright, Constable, and Nathaniel Page, Burleyman, ffor Bridge Trafford.

"Wee present the Baileife of the Court for not giving Bridge Trafford sufficient notice for the appearance at this Court, the sum of 1s.

We present Richard Thomason, for not removing his midding and cleansing his watercourse in the Northgate-street, and doe Amercie him in the sum of 3s. 4d.,

We present the Deane and Charter for not repairing the Courthouse; and also for a Dunghill before the Register office, and we do Amercie them in 13s. 4d.

We present Mrs. Swift, Widdow, for suffering p'te of her house in the Abbey Court, w'ch she holds from the Deane and Chapter, to goe to Ruine and decay; and

Chester Cathedral

we order her to repaire the same before the next Court Leet to be held for this Manner, upon paine of Six pound."

From another Roll dated April, 1695, we glean the following:-

We p'ssnt the Deane and Chapter for not keeping the Stocks in repaire, and amerce them in one shilling.

We p'sent John Bentley and Samuel Rimmer for not repairing the Highway in the Windy mill Lane, to the Comon nuzance, and amerce them in five shillings.

Wee order that Mrs. Elizabeth Swift doe keep the Comon Well in the Abbey Court duely inclosed, to p'vent the danger of p'sons being drowned or hurt in the s'd Well, upon paine of twenty shillings.

One charm of these entries is the admirable impartiality shewn by the Jury. Not only do the simple Township-men of Trafford get pounced upon for not 'mending their ways,' and the poor 'Baileife' of the Court get mulcted for neglect, but even still higher game fails to get off scot free. Thus we see Mrs. Swift, the 'bruar's wife' of that day, - and the representative of those who upon the same spot were such a scandal and eyesore to Bishop Bridgeman and the Archbishop threatened and fined for not performing the covenants of her lease: the Dean and Chapter also. the lords paramount of the Court, come in for their due share both of blame and amerciament.

One of these quaint entries shews that the Chapter had set up Stocks of their own to punish the refractory within their domain. Another entry, not included in the list, shews also that they had a Cuck-stool for ducking any scolds who, within their bailiwick of Boughton, made too free with their tongues. Doubtless many other curious entries are contained in these tell-tale Court Rolls, but enough has for the present been said.
T. HUGHES

Consistory Court Chester Cathedral

35

The Bridge of Sighs

EIGHTEENTH CENTURY

LIST OF CONTENTS:

CAROUSAL AND DUEL AT CHESTER

The following curious details of an inquest held at Chester shortly after the accession of George the Second, will be read with interest. We met with the document in a bundle of inquisitions preserved among ancient muniments of the Corporation of Chester.

"Inquisic'on taken in the Common Hall of Pleas of the said City, before William Hughes, Alderman, and Thomas Brock, Alderman, his Ma'ty's Coroners for the County of the said City on Thursday, the twenty-eight day of September, 1727, upon sight of the dead body of Thomas Robinson, late of the City of Dublin, in the kingdom of Ireland, gentl'n, upon the oaths of thirteen jurors, good and lawful men of the said city, who being charged to enquire by what means the said Thomas Robinson came to his death, Do say upon their oaths that the s'd Thomas Robinson upon Tuesday, the twenty-sixth day of this instant September, in the evening of the same day came into the Golden Talbot Inn, in the Eastgate Street of the said City, in company with one Robert Meredith, gentle'n, and some other gentlemen, upon their Arrival from Dublin, and there supped together; and after supper continued drinking there till ab't two or three of the clock the next morning; in which time some words happened between the s'd Thomas Robinson and ye s'd Rob't Meredith, occasioned by the s'd Thomas Robinson; who afterwards assaulted the s'd Robert Meredith by striking him upon the breast with his head, and then challenged him to fight with him, and layd hold of him, and furnished him with a sword, and took him by the arm, and obliged him to go along with him into the Foregate Street of the s'd City; where the s'd Thomas Robinson and Robert Meredith drew their swords, and the s'd Thomas Robinson made several passes at the s'd Robert Meredith, and wounded him in several places.

And the s'd Jurors upon their oaths say that whilst the s'd Robert Meredith and the s'd Thomas Robinson were engaged in fight as af'd, one John Carrick, gentln., who was then and there present, interposed with his sword drawn, and therewith struck upon the swords of the s'd Robert Meredith and Thomas Robinson endeavouring to beat them down; whereupon instantly the s'd Robert Meredith being upon his own defence, gave the said Thomas Robinson one mortal wound with the sword, w'ch he then and there held in his right Hand, in the left side of his throat, of w'ch s'd wound he languished till ab't eleven of the clock in the last night, and then dyed of the same wound in the s'd City.

And so, the s'd Jrry say that the s'd Robert Meredith did wound and kill the s'd Thomas Robinson, in manner and form af'd, and not otherwise to the knowledge of ye s'd Jury or any of them, or by any Evidence to them appearing. And the s'd Jurors further say that the s'd sword is of the value of one shilling, and is now in the Custody of the Clerk of the Peace of ye s'd City of Chester.

In Testimony whereof, as well the s'd Coroners as the s'd Jurors, have hereunto put their hands and seals, the day and the year first above written.
Signed (and sealed) by the Jurors, and by
WILL'M HUGHES
THO. BROCKE   ~ Coroners"

Alderman Hughes, we may presume, was a Jacobite at heart for he seals with one of the posies of the so-called Pretender, "a crown between a rose and thistle, and the motto contracted, SEM. EA (for Semper eadem). Alderman Brock seals with his own family crest, "a demi-lion reguardant, holding in his right hand a dart".

There were under the Charter two Coroners of the City, a rule which prevailed until our own times.
EDITOR

A WOMAN BURNT AT THE STAKE FOR MURDER

At what particular date the punishment of "Burning at the Stake" for Murder was abolished by statute I am unable to state with any certainty. But I have it upon record that the last instance within our own county of Chester occurred about 120 years ago, at Gallows Hill,

Boughton, in this city, when Mary Heald, Quakoress, suffered that extreme penalty of the law for the murder of her husband. The first official intimation I find of it in the Chester Chronicle *for October, 1762, where it is recorded that:*

"Mary Heald, of Mere, charged upon oath of having poisoned Samuel Heald, her husband, was committed to Chester Castle, by George Heron, Eq., on the 23rd of October, 1762."

The affair created intense interest and excitement at Chester; and hundreds of persons, through the winter of 1762, sought and obtained permission to Visit the dungeon in our old Castle in which the unhappy woman was confined, the gaolers, &c., taking large amounts as largesse for permitting the wretched exhibition. And this sort of thing (and worse still I fear) went on and was winked at by the authorities, until the Easter of 1763, when the County Assizes came on at Chester Castle, I again take up my parable from the Chester Courant, *where I read as follows under date, Chester, April 10 [1763].*

"Last week ended the assize here, when Mary Heald, widow of Samuel Heald, late of Mere, near Knutsford, in this county, yeoman (both of the people called Quakers), was convicted of Petit Treason, in killing her said husband, after twenty years cohabitation; by giving him a certain quantity of arsonick, in a mess of fleetings, on the nineteenth day of October last : of which poison he died, in about four days after taking the same. For which crime she was condemned to he burned, on the day after sentence; but upon application to the judges, they were pleased to respite her execution until Saturday, the 23'd of this instant."

I suppose in this interval of four only days certain benevolent efforts were put forth to try and save the life of the convict but if so, and whatever they were, they failed for on the Market Day following the two Sheriffs of Chester City had most uncongenial work upon their hands, as the following paragraph from the Courant gravely assures us:-
Chester, April 26

"In our last *Courant* were mentioned the trial and condemnation of Mary Heald as also, that the judges had been pleased to respite her execution until Saturday, the 23'd inst. Accordingly, soon after ten of the clock in the forenoon of that day, the sheriffs of Chester, with their attendants, came to Gloverstone. where the gaoler of the Castle deliver'd to them the said Mary Heald; who, pursuant to sentence, was drawn from thence in a sledge, through the city to Spital Boughton; where after due time having been allowed for her private devotion, she was affixed to a stake, on the north side of great road, almost opposit to the gallows and having been first strangled, faggots, pitch barrels, and other combustibles, were properly placed all around her, and the fire being lighted up, her body was consumed to ashes. This unhappy woman behaved with much decency, and left an authentick written declaration, confessing her crime and expressing much penitence and contrition."

The Gentlemen's Magazine *for April, 1763, has a paragraph to the same effect, but much less full than the local report given above. The same Paper contains a Letter from a respectable tradesman of Chester, who I doubt not was an eye-witness to the whole affair, and whose testimony to the humanity of the Sheriffs in the performance of their distressing duty is worth reproducing here :-*

"To the Mayor, Recorder, Justices of the Peace, and Sheriffe of the City of Chester.

Your tender regard relating to the execution of the unfortunate Mary Heald on the 23'd instant, justly merits an acknowledgment in a public manner, be pleased to accept it in such. The concern of many of you at the poor criminal's unhappy fate, and the care you took in preserving the peace, is highly commendable in the eye of every impartial spectator. The stillness and decency wherewith the execution was conducted by the Sheriffs, will continue, on many minds, an instance of their candour and great humanity. I am, on this particular occasion, with great regard and esteem, Your much obliged Friend,
PETER LEADBETTER
April 26, 1763."

Mr. Leadbetter was in error in addressing this laudatory letter to the Mayor, Recorder or Justices for they had no authority whatever in the matter. It was the duty of the Sheriffs alone to see execution done; and they would have resented any interference with their prerogative, by either Mayor or Justices. Even the executioner, the guard accompanying the convict, and keeping the peace round the gallows, were all the Sheriffs officers for the time being, and were paid by them. This questionable privilege of our Shrieval forefathers has now ceased, and the High Sheriff of the County is solely responsible for vindicating in that sense, the majesty of the law. I close this lamentable narrative with the reprint of a hand-bill of the period, and now in my collection, in which the "authentik written" Confession of the poor woman, shortly prior to her execution, is given at length.

The Confession of Mary Heald, late of Mere Town, in Cheshire, who was burned at Chester, the 23rd day of April, 1763, for poisoning her Husband.

"I was born in the Parish of Alderley in Cheshire, My Parents at the Time of my Birth (and for some years atterwards) were Members of the Church of England. In my childhood my Parents went amongst the people called Quakors, and educated me and their other children in that way.

Amongst the People I was married to my late Husband, Samuel Heald; but, unhappily, in a short time after our Marriage, Uneasiness grew between us, and, for want of Watchfulness, it increased to a very great degree. Several of the Society from time to time visited, and advised us to a better conduct. I am now very sensible of their sure and kindness therein, and happy it had been for me if I had duly regarded their good Advice and Council, and the Convictions of Divine grace in my own Heart. But alas! I disregarded them, and having given myself up to Rage and Passion against my Husband, was tempted to take away his Life; into which dreadful Temptation I was suffered to fall, after this manner.

One day, going into his Desk to take a little sugar, I found some Poison in a little paper, which I took, and intended to burn it, but did not, but kept it in my custody some weeks; when one Day, having a strong Temptation to give it my Husband, I put it into a Mess of Fleetings, which, he eating of, caused his Death, for which horrible Cruelty and Wickedness I am now justly to suffer death.

I am deeply sensible of the Heinousness of the crime I have been guilty of, which no one was concerned [in], or knew of, but myself; and I desire no Reflections may be cast on any Persons after am dead, as it was my own Act! I have grievously sinned against God and Man: May my dreadful example be a Caution and Warning to all (especially married people), that they guard against the first Entrance of Anger and Passion into their Minds one against another! Oh, may the God of Mercy, who regarded the thief on the cross, grant unto me the Grace of sincere Repentance, thro' the Mediation and Intercession of His beloved Son, Jesus Christ, for this heinous Sin, and all my other Trespasses and Sins that i have committed against Him, that when my sentence is executed, my soul may be received into Rest!

The "M" mark of Mary Heald."

T. HUGHES

PENANCE FOR DEFAMATION

Among the many terrors to evil sayers and doers with which old Chester at one time swarmed, the Ecclesiastical Court and its ill-assorted penalties held a prominent place. It had its own stern officials, its own rigid code, it had it's own darksome prison. It's judge condemned slanderers to penance, martyrs to the stake and the Sheriffs of the City or County, as the case might be, had to see execution done, without liberty of appeal or evasion. There the defamer of other men, the openly immoral of life, the free thinker in religion, the profane swearer, nay even the unfit and unlicensed schoolmaster, were mercilessly arraigned, and there paid the certain penalty of their misdeeds.

The following Record, found recently among the Sheriff's Papers of Chester city, will afford an example of the means adopted to bring defiant offenders to justice. The Sheriff's of the city, as we shall see, were called upon and compelled to give the coup de grace to a wretched wight whose tongue had proved a trifle too large for his slanderous mouth.

"George The Third, by the Grace of God of Great Britain, ffrance, and Ireland, King, Defender of the Faith, and so forth, - To the Sheriffs of the City of Chester, Greeting.

Whereas Edmund, by Divine permission, Lord Bishop of Chester, hath Signified to us that Abel Ward, clerk Master of Arts, the lawful Surrogate of the Reverend and Worshipful Samuel Peploe, rightly, lawfully, and judicially proceeding by Our Ordinary Authority, did Pronounce Thomas Williams of the Parish of Saint Oswald, in the City and Diocese of Chester, Husbandman, to be Contumacious for his manifest Contempt for the Law and Ecclesiastical Jurisdiction in not appearing before our said Vicar General, his lawful Surrogate in our Consistory Court within the Cathedral Church of Chester at a certain time in that behalf prefixed, and now past, and extracting in due form of Law a certain Order or Declaration of Penance heretofore enjoined him to be performed by Our definitive Sentence or final Decree given and pronounced against him in a certain cause or business of speaking certain Scandalous, Reproachfull, and defamatory words of and against Ann Morphett, the Wife of Edward Morphett, of the same parish, Husbandman, namely, that she was a _____ and also for not paying or causing to be paid to the Party of the said Ann Morphett the Sum of Six Pounds of good and lawfull money of Great Britain for her expenses in the said cause or business, and by the said Surrogate lawfully Taxed, together with the sum of Fifteen Shillings and eight pence of her money for the fees of Two Monitions issued against him for the payment thereof on or before the twenty-fourth day of April last, And in pain of this his Contempt, &e., to be Excommunicated with the greater Excommunication; and on the third Day of May last did cause him, the said Thomas Williams, &c., to be Excommunicated by a Schedule in writing, read by a Priest; and to be publicly denounced and declared so to be in the fface of the congregation assembled in time of divine service in the Parish Church of St. Oswald, on Sunday, the ffourth day of May aforesaid. Yet this notwithstanding, the said Thomas Williams, for 40 days past since the said Excommunication, both persisted, &c. and doth obstinately, persist under the same, wickedly despising his exclusion from the communion of the Church, to the great danger of his own Soul and Evil Example of others. And whereas the Ecclesiastical Law, &c., have it not in their power to proceed further against him;

Wherefore we command you to apprehend and imprison the said Thomas Williams by his Body, and until he shall have fully Satisfied the Holy Church as well touching the Contempt as the Injury done thereto by him, And what you shall do in the promises certify to our Justices of Chester, at Chester, upon the first day of the next Sessions for the County of Chester, at Chester, &e. Witness oneself at Chester, the Sixth Day of December, in the Seventh year of our reign. (1767)"

Salusbury Brereton
R. BAXTER

The dread of the "white sheet" had begun to loose its grip on the popular mind, even in Charles the First's days, as our local annals curiously prove to us; though there have been one or two examples of its use within our own times that were, as the petrel's visits, only presaging the certain storm. A few years only passed, and the Ecclesiastical Court with it's clumsy pains, penalties, and imprisonments, vanished finally from view, never in our days to reappear.
G. T.

CONSPIRACY AT CHESTER GAOL

The Annual Register of March, 1767, *says;-*

"A conspiracy was formed among the felons in the North gate Jail of Chester, wherin one Evan Thomas, who was confined for murder and robbery, was the ring leader about eight, when the turnkey was going to put him and three others into the dungeon, Thomas seized him, and threw him into the dungeon and took the key from him and locked him in. his cries brought Mr. Whitehead, the gaoler, down to his assistance, when Thomas ran a pen-knife into his throat, and killed him on the spot. They went up into the house, and seizing Mrs. Whitehead, demanded the key of the North Gate from her, who told them that her husband had it in his pocket; upon which they went down stairs to look for it. In the meantime Mrs. Whitehead unlocked the northgate door, to call assistance; but they came up again and seized her while the door was open; three men, however, coming out of the street secured three of the felons, but Evan Thomas made his escape. His irons were found the next day in a field near the city."

Further issues of the magazine are silent as to Evan Thomas's fate.
Croeswylan, Oswestry.
A. R.

EXECUTION IN CHESTER, 1771

The following extract from a letter dated Chester, Sept. 7, 1771, appears in the Annual Register for that year:-

"The following is an account of John Chapman, who was executed here for robbing Martha Hewitt, of this county. At the hour appointed he was conducted to the place of execution by a greater number of constables than usual, as there was some suspicion of a rescue by the vast concourse of sailers (he being one of that profession) that accompanied him. On his setting out, a book was put into his hand by the hangman, which he no sooner received than he threw among his brother shipmates, as he termed them; and they immediately tore it to pieces. A clergyman got into the cart, and exhorted him to behave with more decency, and to think of his sudden change; but instead of attending to this admonition, he got up in the cart, and (being pinioned) drove his head in the clergyman's belly, and tumbled him out of the cart :- After this he flung himself out, and attempted to run into the midst of the sailors, but was prevented by the irons with which he was loaded :- he was then seized and tied by ropes in the cart, and in that manner tied to the fatal tree :- at his arrival there he refused either to hear prayers or to pray himself ; therefore two men, together with the hangman, attempted to lift him up, to fix the rope about his neck, in doing of which, he by some means got the hangman's thumb in his mouth, which he almost separated from the hand: he was at last tied up, but with great difficulty."

The foregoing is not "original matter of value" to which you wisely announce you give preference; but failing contributions of that kind this may be worth binding in your Sheaf *as a specimen of bye-gone times.*

Croeswylan, Oswestry.
A. R.

THE PILLORY AT CHESTER

Dr. Brushfield, in his article on the Pillory at the above reference, quotes the following entry as in the Treasurers Annual Accounts of the Corporation of Chester:-

"1771, April 27. Paid twelve constables by Mr. Mayor's order for attending whilst Mary Axson stood in the pillory: 12s. 0d."

I should like to know what was poor Axon's *offence, for which she was adjudged to the pillory at Chester High Cross 112 years ago? And came it that twelve constables were required to keep her, or perhaps the crowd around her, in order ? Had she been a "scold," she would have received different treatment, for our great-grandfathers knew the great virtue of the iron brank to "bridle a woman's tongue." I'm afraid, from what I now and then read in the papers, that there still live some of my sex to whom the administration of the brank might prove an efficient if not an over agreeable cure. "Let*

the women keep silence, &c. !"
Birkenhead.
LUCY D. T.

***Watergate Street &
Watergate Rows***

THE PUPPET SHOW EXPLOSION, 1772

A hundred and seven years ago this day, here happened the most terrible calamity ever recorded in our Chester annals. The gabled front of the premises where the accident occurred is still standing, next door but three to the westward of Bishop Lloyd's House, in Watergate Street; and the passage at its side, leading into Commonhall Street, still bears popularly the name of the Puppet Show Entry The Chester Courant of Nov. 10, says:-

42

"On November the 5th, a few minutes before nine o'clock in the evening, the inhabitants of this city were greatly alarmed by a loud unusual noise, attended with a shaking of the ground, which everyone imagined to proceed from an earthquake. But the news soon arrived that a large number of people, assembled at a puppet-show, had been blown up by gunpowder, placed in a grocer's warehouse which was under the room. Amidst the universal consternation and confusion occasioned by this dreadful calamity, it happened most fortunately that some gentlemen had repaired to the melancholy scene a few minutes after the accident; who gave particular directions that every person who showed the least sign of life should be immediately carried to the Infirmary, where the physicians and surgeons would be ready to administer every possible means of relief. The number admitted that night was 33, and 20 since, in all 53. Besides 23 dead, and these 53 Hospital patients, there appear to be about 30 more in the town who received some degree of injury, in the shape of light contusions and burns,- in all about 106."

I have searched the files in the City Muniment room at the Town Hall, and have come upon the original Inquisition held on the dead bodies found in the ruins. It runs as follows:-

"City of Chester and County of the same City - to wit.

An Inquisition taken at the Inner Pentice of the said City of Chester, on Saturday, the Seventh day of November, in the 13th year of the Reign of our Sovereign Lord, George the third, King of Great Britain, &c., in the year of our Lord, 1772 before Thomas Craven, one of his Majesty's Coroners for the County of the City of Chester aforesaid, upon sight of the Dead Bodys of (here follows a list of the dead) Upon the Oath of (here follows a list of jurors) good and Lawful Men of the County of the said City; who being charged to inquire how and by what means the several persons before mentioned, now lying dead, came to their Death, Do say upon their Oath, That the several Persons hereinbefore Particularly

named and described on the fifth day of this Instant November, being assembled with divers other Persons in a certain Room, called "Eaton's Room", situate in the Watergate Street, in the said City, to see a Puppet Show, were blown up and killed by the Accidental Explosion of some gunpowder which was Deposited in a Warehouse under the said Room. And the Jurors aforesaid upon their Oath aforesaid Say, That the several persons herein before mentioned and described came to their Death by Accident and the Means aforesaid....."

Funeral Sermons were preached in the various churches and chapels of the city, and a Poem (now very scarce) was written and published in commemoration of the sad event. A large sum of money was raised for the relief of the sufferers and the family of the deceased.
T. HUGHES

BALLS AND BALL-GOERS A CENTURY AGO

The following extracts from the Chester Guide and Directory, *Chester: printed and sold by J. Broster, in the Exchange also sold T. Longman, Paternoster Row, London, and by all the News Carriers, 1782, may be interesting to your readers, and especially to such of them as have lately enjoyed the Winter Balls at the Grosvenor Hotel, and also to those learned barristers and grand jurymen who have been engaged at the recent Assizes. The present ball room at the Grosvenor Hotel formed part of the New Assembly Rooms of the Talbot mentioned in these extracts. Fortunately, through a legal difficulty, it was not taken down when the old buildings were removed to make room for the present Grosvenor, as there is not a better floor on which to dance in the kingdom:-*

"Inns and Public Houses

There are about 140 inns and public-houses. The principal inns are the White Lion, in Northgate street, where the post coaches and machines come to.

The Talbot, in Eastgate street, adjoining to which are the New Assembly Rooms, built by subscription in 1777.

The Card Assembly, every Monday, and to begin at five o'clock. Dancing Assembly, every other Monday, and to begin at seven.

That the subscription to the Winter Assemblies be, to gentlemen, one guinea and a half; ladies, fifteen shillings.

That non-subscribers resident in town, do pay for admission to the Dancing Assemblies, gentlemen, three shillings and sixpence, and one shilling for tea; ladies, two shillings and sixpence, and sixpence for tea.

Card Assemblies, gentlemen, one shilling and sixpence, and one shilling for tea; ladies, one shilling and six pence, and sixpence for tea.

That strangers and non-residents do pay for admission to the Dancing Assembly, two shillings and six pence gentlemen paying one shilling, and ladies six pence, for tea.

Card Assembly, One shilling; gentlemen and ladies paying sixpence [each] for tea.

That ladies and gentlemen choosing to dance on the Card Assembly nights do pay for the winter, gentlemen, five shillings; ladies, two shillings and sixpence.

Non-subscribers to pay for each night, gentlemen, one shilling; ladies, sixpence.

That a ticket, admitting a lady or gentleman to the Assemblies at the Races. be for three nights, half a guinea; four nights, half a guinea and half a crown; five nights, fifteen shillings. Non-Subscribers to pay five shillings for each night. Gentlemen to pay one shilling, and ladies sixpence, for tea.

That admittance to each Assize Ball be, to gentlemen, three shillings and sixpence; ladies, two shillings and sixpence gentlemen paying one shilling for tea, ladies paying sixpence, for tea.

Among the other inns were the Yacht Inn, in Watergate street, and the Plume of Feathers in Bridge street.

Rates of Chairmen.

For every set down from any part of this city or liberties thereof, within the distances after mentioned:- (s.d.)
To the May-pole in further Northgate street:-0.6.
To the May-pole in Handbridge:-0.6.
To Mr. Brock's House without the Bars:-0.6.
To any Houses without the Watergate, and within the Crane:-0.6.
To any houses by Dee-side as far as Mrs. Kenrick's [now Aikman's] Garden:-0.6. Double fare:-1.0.

For every set-down within the liberties of this city beyond the above limits:-1.0.
Double fare:-2.0.
For waiting the first hour:-1.0.
For every hour afterwards:-0.9.

The hours of waiting to be from nine o'clock in the morning until twelve at night, at the several places where the chairmen usually stand, or at their respective dwelling houses.

At all Assemblies, Balls, Plays, or other public nights, where the chairmen attend, they are to range their chairs in a line, to take each their fare in rotation as they come upon the stand, and to continue plying until half an hour past twelve o'clock.

The chairmen cannot engage their chairs, or keep them in waiting for any particular person on any of the above nights.

If a chair he sent for to any house and brought at the time appointed without being used, the person sending for it is to pay sixpence in lieu of a fare.

Every person sending for a chair, and keeping it above a quarter of an hour before using it, shall pay a fare of one shilling.

The chairmen to attend any house or place where desired, unless they are engaged in carrying any other person.

The chairs are to be numbered, and the name of the foreman to be painted on the front of each chair.

Chairmen are not to be impertinent or otherwise misbehave themselves. taking more than the above fares, or breaking any of these rules, subjects the chairman to a penalty of five shillings, or to suspension for such time as the commissioners shall think fit."
Curzon Park.
H. IAYLOR

THE VOLUNTEERS OF 1783

We have recently seen, in an ordinary Penny serial of the hour, an assumably original narrative of the Chester Volunteers hurried march from this City to Delamere Forest in 1783, on the news suddenly arriving here that a hostile force had just encamped on that then unenclosed district. Though a prize of a guinea has been awarded for the article, it is only right to the original author to record that the story was printed at Chester more than a half century ago; and that Joseph Hemingway wrote it, editor of the Chester Chronicle, *who wrote it, included it in the second volume of his published* History of Chester *pp. 250, 8vo. 1831. In honour of our deceased historian we here give the story in his own words:-*

"It is no disparagement to the most renowned military men that they do not fight, when no enemy dares to present itself in the field before them. had the Frenchmen presumed to approach our shores in a hostile attitude, there is no doubt but the Chester Volunteers of that day would have covered themselves with glory; and that they did not thus approach was no fault of theirs. Although these brave men were disappointed in meeting a foreign enemy, an occurrence most fortunate for their credit furnished an opportunity for showing their prowess; and as this military exploit has never been recorded in the gazette, it shall have a place here.

Towards the close of the American war, a numerous and lawless banditti associated together for the purposes of plunder, in the vicinity of Chester; who by their nocturnal depredations, the whole neighbourhood into a state of constant trepidation and alarm, while, by the well-managed secrecy of their movements, their place of rendezvous remained undiscoverable to the ken of the civil authorities. At length, however, a noted thief of the name of Bebbington was apprehended for a criminal offence, and lodged in the Northgate prison, he was shrewdly suspected of being one of the dangerous gang; and the sly rogue, either with a view of passing a mischievous hoax, or in the hopes of benefiting himself, seemed disposed to favour the suspicion. The capture of this fellow was thus considered of the highest importance, as no doubt existed but he could give such information as might lead to the apprehension of his confederates. On being pressed to a disclosure, Bebbington at first affected some scrupulosity; and then, as if yielding to a sense of duty, assured the magistrates, that the marauders were exceedingly numerous, that their purposes were of the most dangerous nature,- that a sense of danger had rendered them quite desperate, and that it would require an overwhelming force to capture them and at the same time describing with minute precision the particular places of their concealment on the edge of the Forest [of Delamere], and about Kelsall.

A consultation of the magistracy was immediately called, and a resolution entered into to storm the enemy's camp. But the enterprise was deemed too formidable, without the aid of the military; the Commandant of the Volunteers was applied to, who instantly offered the services of his gallant band: and as a night attack was deemed the most effective, in the afternoon of the same day, the drums beat to arms, and in little more than an hour's time, the whole corps was mustered in marching order, fully equipped for the field, to the number of about one hundred and twenty, rank and file. The expedition was a secret one, and as few either of the men or inhabitants knew its destination, a thousand rumours spread as to its object; some affirming one and some another, but all agreeing in this, that the service was of the most perilous and important kind! Appalling lamentations were heard in every quarter: and when the word march was given, and while the corps wended their steps through the streets, the piercing cries and sobs of wives, children, sisters, sweethearts and friends, were truly pitiable - all apparently auguring that they should see their faces no more!

The route was towards the forest, and it was now no longer necessary to conceal the fact that they were destined to act against a numerous and desperate band of armed robbers. It was in the depth of winter, the roads were ankle-deep in mud, and ere they had well cleared the suburbs of the city, the shades of night had closed in upon them. The historian is not informed that, at this stage of the expedition. a single ejaculation on the hardships of a soldier's life had escaped the lips of officer or private, such was their ardour for martial glory. To relieve the fatigues of a long march, Stamford Bridge presented a very suitable place for a halt; where, without the aid of a foraging party, "the sign-post caught the passing eye," and where courage and good resolution were rewarded and sustained, with almost every drop of beverage that the village could furnish. Arriving at Tarvin, an equally courageous assault was made on the stock of every

Boniface there; and if report may be credited, not even the remnant of a barrel or bottle remained to cheer the passing traveller on his way. It has been said, that several distinguished instances of bravery were manifested in this village; but as the particulars have not been authoritatively recorded, we shall pass them over with this slightest notice. The brave little army, however, full of spirits soon arrived near the scene of conflict, and they approached the village of Kelsall (where their operations were to commence) with great circumspection, the commander-in-chief having issued his orders with consummate skill.

The first post to be assailed was a dwelling-house situated at bite end of the village, in which, were said to be concealed considerable numbers of the banditti, with immense quantities of booty, arms and ammunition; and nothing could

Chester Castle

exceed the dispositions made for the assault, nor the promptness and precision with which the orders of the commander were executed. In a very short time the fortress was surrounded, and a summons proclaimed by a violent knock at the door, and a demand for surrender at discretion. This was several times repeated without effect; when just as the orders to storm were about to be given, a feeble voice from within was heard, imploring mercy and protection, the door at the same time being thrown open. The house was instantly filled with soldiers, those in the rear and flank having received strict orders not to suffer any of the enemy to escape in those directions. The concealed thieves and booty were demanded with great sternness; while a poor old woman, the only human being visible in the house, almost petrified with fear, wrung her hands, exclaiming,

"O gentlemen, I never thought it would come to this; bless you! don't take him away; he will marry her, indeed he will!"

This inexplicable appeal rather increased than allayed suspicion, and they proceeded to search the premises. After diligent inquisition, they found a young country fellow, stretched on the floor under a bed; whom they dragged forth, half dead with fear, and who, on being interrogated, could be brought to no other answer than that "he would marry her".

Recourse now being had to several other persons in the village, the result was found to be that the supposed harbour for thieves and the magazine for booty, was the residence of a quiet old widow of good repute that the countryman whom they had seized as a prisoner, was her son; that he was acquainted with a young woman in a neighbouring parish, whom he had shown some repugnance to marry; and that both the widow and her son, supposing the attack upon the house to be connected with a design of the parish officers to take him to prison, had both of them given an assurance that "he would marry her!"

Two or three other places on the borders of the forest had been described by Bebbington as retreats of the banditti; but the deception in the above instance seems to have abated their credulity or cooled their military ardour. It was now past midnight, and in the depth of winter they were seven or eight miles from home, without quarters ; and withal many of them the worse for their stimulating libations.

Their military exploit being accomplished, there seemed no further necessity for military discipline; they grouped together in twos, threes, or half dozens, as chance or inclination dictated. The first of the returning victors did not reach Chester till after day light next morning. and many of the rear not till towards evening. An awful suspense pervaded the city during the preceding night; and before the appearance of day terrific rumours were general, that the gallant band had encountered a numerous enemy in Delamere Forest and were cut to pieces. It is gratifying, however, to say, that notwithstanding the danger and severity of the service, not a life was lost. Two or three of hardy veterans only are [1831] now living; who still recount with much glee and good humour the glories of that eventful night. It may just be added, that the wily Bebbington afterwards succeeded in detaching a posse of the civil power into Wirral, in quest of the rogues, where he pretended they were assembled: but this, like the former, proved a sheer hoax."

Of course the story had at the its ludicrous side: and no doubt the little band of Chester Volunteers, on their return home after their fruitless errand, had to endure plenty of unwelcome chaff from the courageous sparks who, with an inward sense of tremor, saw them march away on their patriotic errand, yet who felt themselves the bravest of the brave in staying behind, safe within their ancient walls. But it is just as well to remember that no one then in Chester for a moment disbelieved the sudden rumour; that the Volunteers was as prompt on that day, as their great grandsons were a century afterwards, to fly to the post of duty at the mandate of authority and that one hundred drilled men at such an hour of

47

need would make short work of a thousand raw and inexperienced rebels against law and order. In this sense the result of that all-night march were not without their value

G. T.

LOCAL FOLKLORE: THE CHESHIRE WIZARD

Dick Spot lived at Whitchurch, Salop, but was, I think, a native of Cheshire. I do not know the date of his death, but fancy it must have been early in the present century. It was generally believed in the two counties that he practised the "black art." Whatever was lost or stolen, Dick was usually consulted professionally, and things were often restored to their owners in a most mysterious manner, in fact, Dick's name was quite a terror to evil-doers.

During the winter season, a century or so ago, the farm servants of Cheshire were much employed in spinning wool for linsey, to make gowns and petticoats, also linen for household purposes, such as bed-ticks, sheets, table cloths, &c. These were usually put on the grass or garden hedge near the house, to bleach. One night a roll of linen was missing from a grass-pat, familiar enough to me in my younger days. There being no apparent sign of its return, the farmer made known his intention of consulting Dick, who, he said, would make them bring it back over hedges and tops of trees! The delinquent had no notion of being treated in such an unceremonious and repulsive manner, so stealthily replaced the linen where he had found it, which was, of course, just the result that the owner expected and desired.

In Foregate Street, Chester, not far from the Old Royal Oak, lived a bachelor who had placed in a bag £300, and put it, as he thought, safely away in his desk. One day he discovered it was gone. He strongly suspected one of his neighbours, no one else having access to his back premises. He made it known that on a certain day he should go to Whitchurch to consult Dick Spot. He hired a horse from one, borrowed a top coat from another, and fixed five o'clock next morning for his departure. However, that same night, the front door flew open, and the bag was thrown in to the middle of the floor, with the missing money in it, safe and sound!

I once heard a strange story, which I had from an old gentlemen well known in this city. In his younger days he resided in Christleton. Having placed a sum of money amounting to upwards of £200, in his desk there, he went away from home after having safely locked up his house. On his return, he found his money gone. He went off at once to Dick, who said, "Go to an inn for the night; I will see what I can do in the morning." He accordingly did so. Next morning Dick said, "Thou will't never get a farthing back it is all spent." Dick then brought a glass, such as Doctor Dee is represented to have used in his day, bidding him look into it, He did so, and saw, as he believed the face of a man well-known to him, in fact a near neighbour. Dick then asked him if he remembered one Sunday night reading the Bible and going to sleep, the Bible falling to the floor, and then his suddenly awaking to see a man getting out of the window? Dick stated, without hesitation, that that was the man! He remembered the circumstance well, exactly as Dick had stated to him, and nothing was afterwards heard of the money; doubtless only another evidence to his mind of the wonderful knowledge of the Cheshire wizard! belief in sorcery is still a long way from extinct among the lower orders of the county.

POLYANTHUS

Dick Spot may have lived at Whitchurch, in common with many other places, for he was much given to moving about; but Oswestry was his chief dwelling place and at Oswestry he was buried. He died on the 8th March, 1793, at the age of 83. A pamphlet Life of him was published with the following title:-

"The Life and Mysterious Transactions of Richard Morris, Esq., better known by the name of Dick spot the Conjuror; particularly in Derbyshire and

Shropshire; written by an old Acquaintance who was a critical observer of all his actions for neare fifty years, &c. London, 1798."

Morris was stated to have been born in Bakewell, in Derbyshire, in 1710. He obtained the name of "Dick Spot" in consequence of his having a black spot on his face. He was a handy mechanic, and the life states there was a clock, of his making and invention, at the White Horse, Frankwell, Shrewsbury.

Mr. Hulbert mentions Dick Spot in his History of Shropshire; *and Mr. Randall of Madeley, in* The Salopian *Illustrated Journal he published in (September, 1876), narrates an amusing instance of a rustic going to visit the "Wise Mon of Hodgistry" from the Wenlock district. There have been several references to him in* Bye-gones. *There are two grandsons (cousins) of Morris's living at the present-time in Oswestry; one (who is better known as "Spot" than his proper name), a jockey and (when sober) clever steeplechase rider.*
Croeswylan, Oswestry.
A. R.

RAISING THE DEVIL

Among the Cheshire Broadsides collected during a long life by the late Edward Hawkins, Esq., Keeper of the Antiquities in the British Museum, was the following curious fly-sheet relating to a catastrophe at Tranmere, resulting from an impious and infamous piece of folly there enacted. There is no date to the Broadsheet, but it may be presumed from the type, paper, &c, to come within the years 1780-1820

Full and particular account of the Awful Visitation of The Devil and Six of his Monsters Which appeared to a party of Young Women foolishly and wickedly calling upon them to appear in the form of their intended Bride-grooms, at Tranmere, on All Hallow Eve.

Sorry are we to record another of those scandalous and wicked practices of young people calling upon the Devil to appear unto them in the form of their intended husbands or wives. There have

been for those many years back fatal accidents happening on the night of All Hallowed Eve, through this improper conduct.

It is really astonishing that, in this enlightened age we are in, people cannot employ their time, a thing so precious in this world, in trying to obtain the happiness of the next, instead of drawing down the just judgement of God upon their wicked heads, through their own impiety. Had the persons to whom we are alluding, instead of thus wickedly amusing themselves on the fatal night, have read a few chapters in the Bible, they would, in all probability, have escaped the judgement which has befallen them. The following are the particulars:-

Yesterday being the Eve of All Saints, Sarah Mosely and Ann Lewis, living at service in the house of Mr. Harris, Tranmere, invited several of their acquaintances to their master's house to spend the evening, having gained his consent on the evening previous.

The master and mistress retired to rest about eleven o'clock, leaving the servants and their company to enjoy themselves as long as they thought proper. After perhaps drinking freely of the juice of grapes, besides other little nick-snacks in that way, they consented to try a scheme, the intention, of which was to endeavour to see the faces of their intended lovers. They accordingly commenced by laying a table out with all the necessaries of life, with 5 chairs round it (there being five of them in company): then they read the Lord's Prayer backwards, at the conclusion of which they hoped In the name of his Satanic Majesty, that their intended bridegrooms, would come and seat themselves at the table! No sooner had they uttered this, than their wish was complied with: it being about the hour of twelve, the doors flew open, and in an instant five ghastly looking gentlemen were seated round the table!!

The young women's fright was now heightened to a considerable degree at the sight of so awful a set of beings. They sat for little more than half an hour, when they arose, made their "obedience," and disappeared as they came. Sarah Mosely was so much frightened that she died this morning, and little hopes are entertained of the recovery of the remainder."

I have been unable to trace the burial of this wretched woman: the Rev. G.R. Frilden, Rector of Bebington in which parish Tranmere is situated, informs me she was not buried there.
G. T.

WIFE SELLING

The infamous custom of Wife Selling in open market has recently received a fitting check from the magistrates of a not very distant borough. The following extract from the Chester Chronicle *of April 24, 1799, supplies an instance of the custom, which, it may be hoped, is almost unique in local annals:-*

"The men of Cheshire have often signalised themselves in the annals of courage and gallantry; an additional instance of which occurred a few days ago at Macclesfield, in this county, where an honest farmer actually purchased the wives of two of his neighbours, in the public market: for one of whom he gave half a crown, and for the other, one

The Footbridge

shilling. This brace of brides he lead home, their necks gracefully ornamented with halters, and introduced them into the presence of a first wife; where, greater even than Alexander the Great, the farmer enjoys the smiles of his Rival Queens, and, with his Roxana, Statira, and his third Dulcinea, is likely to feel every mark of sincerity from their tender hands which a hero so moderate in his desires, can reasonably wish for. The farmer's name is Twig, a slender sort of appellation for so Herculean an undertaking: and tho' it may signify the pliability of the man's mind, would not (as Hamlet says) "the praise have been more germane to the matter had he been called Oak?"

Wrexham
LANDWOR

The Town Hall

NINETEENTH CENTURY

LIST OF CONTENTS:

OLD OAK COFFIN AT ST. JOHN'S, CHESTER

The perambulating Chester Guides, a race not yet quite extinct, have from time to time made up many a foolish story about this solid Oak Coffin for the delectation of their Lancashire dupes, who usually pay more court to that ghastly old shell than to the beautiful architectural Ruins and Church that adjoin it . One story is that it was the coffin of a monk who murdered one of his brethren at St, John's, and at his own death was refused the ordinary Christian burial, whether within the church or beneath the green sod of the churchyard. Another is that a dignitary of the church was at his own request buried up there in a standing position, so that, when the last trumpet should sound, he might be ready at once to answer the call. Another is that a wicked old parishioner of past days was unable to rest in his grave, and that Satan himself had helped to place him in the lofty position so that he might look down, in perpetual penance, on the fair world he had defiled by his sins. I have overheard during the last dozen years every one of these stories recounted in sober earnest by Mr. Guide to his morbid listeners.

The real story of the Coffin is soon told. Forty years ago, when a boy at school, I remember old John Carter, the then sexton of the Cathedral, going with me at my request into St. John's Ruins (at that time enveloped within a brick wall, and portion of the of the old Priory House), to show me the relic and then fresh-looking inscription. He assured me on the spot that his father, who was sexton of St. John's a great number of years, had in his younger days come upon the Coffin while digging a grave in a long disused part of the churchyard; and had, by the Rector's (Mr. Richardson's) orders, stuck it up in the recess where it still stands, so that it might be out of the way of passers by! Thus has a very matter of fact in incident given rise in superstitious minds to no end of mystery. The date of the coffin is probably of the latter half of the 15th century and the relic has this one element of real interest in it, that it is

composed of a single block of oak which has been hollowed out to receive the body.
G. T.

**The Oak Coffin,
St. John's Church**

PRACTICAL JOKERS IN CHESTER

The very absurdity of the following circumstance coupled with it's local interest, will perhaps secure it a place in The Cheshire Sheaf:-

"In the night of Tuesday, during the late fair at Chester, some person or persons deposited a considerable quantity assafaetida, mixed with oil of hartshoru, or some other offensive ingredient, in the crevices of several shop doors, principally inhabited by linen drapers and clothiers, which rendered the shops so very disagreeable, that business could scarcely be done in them for two days afterwards: many ladies nearly fainted in coming to them, and were obliged to go out immediately."

I transcribe this from The Salopian Journal of October 30, 1805.
Croeswylan, Oswestry
A. R.

A somewhat similar incident, and quite equal to it in folly, took place some seven or eight years ago in the old King's School at Chester. It was the school "Speech Day", and a large number of friends of the institution, and relations of the pupils, had assembled to witness the Presentation of the Prizes.

Before, however, the doors were opened to the public, a brace of young imps had busied themselves in quietly strewing small heaps of a subtle powder here and there about the room,- a work which no one else noticed, and which no one perhaps would have remarked upon, even if he had. The room gradually filled with people, and the proceedings in due course commenced. The Head Master, the late Rev. James Harris, made his customary speech; but little enthusiasm was aroused until the reverend dignitary who occupied the chair made a few good points in his address to the Boys which were vigorously applauded. All at once the audience became excited, they scarcely knew why, and emotion was visible in many a countenance. The Chairman he was making an unusual impression on his hearers, so redoubled his efforts and added fire to his periods. Soon it was noticed that most of those present, the chairman included, were in tears; and it may safely be said that many an eye was red that day with weeping to which tears had indeed for a long time been strangers! The Chairman concluded his moving speech, and in a short while the company departed wondering, nay half ashamed, that their feelings should have so strongly overcome them. I lingered behind to glean the cause of this strange excitement; and it was whispered to me, by one in on the secret, that what the Head Master and The Chairman had regarded as the fruits of their oratory, was in reality but the "dust kicked up" which those two young sinners had scattered so adroitly an hour or so before! Half-a-crown ill spent on cayenne pepper and snuff had brought tears to cheeks which even the eloquence of a Spurgeon would have failed to move!

Of course it was a senseless joke, and ought not to have been perpetrated. But equally of course, such freaks are inherent in the school-boy; and no amount of education or even punishment will ever quite eradicate the love of mischief from the brain of the thoughtless young Englishman.

T. HUGHES

A MATRIMONIAL SQUABBLE

Two little hand-bills, pasted into an old scrap-book now before me, are perhaps the only remaining trace of a domestic difficulty which seventy-five years ago, formed food for gossip in the adjoining township of Hoole. The charge and the rejoinder follow promptly on each other.

"Whereas Sidney Hewitt, my Wife, on the 16th day of March last, in my absence from home, voluntarily and without any just or reasonable cause, eloped from my house, and she hath ever since continued absent therefrom.

This, therefore is to give Notice, To the tradesmen of Chester, and to the public at large, not to give my said Wife any trust or credit whatsoever, as I certainly shall not pay any debt which she shall or may hereafter contract; nor do I hold myself answerable for any debts which she may have already incurred since the time of her elopement aforesaid.

Given under my hand this 3rd day of April, 1805.

THOMAS HEWITT
Hoole-house, near Chester."

"Whereas Thomas Hewit, my husband, put out Hand-bills last night to say, I absconded without a Cause: I, Sidney Hewit, post this to certify that I absconded to save my Life, which he has threatened from Time to Time. As for the Debts he speaks of, I have not incurred any but those that are unavoidable; and I believe the Trades-people of Chester will do me the Justice to say that I never did otherwise.

SIDNEY HEWIT"

The axiom as to the washing of dirty linen away from home seems not to have been regarded much at Hoole at the beginning of this century! The parties concerned were persons of some consideration, at the date of this matrimonial dispute and separation.

H. S. A.

HARE HUNT IN THE STREETS OF CHESTER

The circumstance of another hare being hunted through the streets of the old city is very remarkable, and well worthy of being placed as a 'new ear' in The Sheaf, occurring as it does so close to the same day of the year with the one previously chronicled; the former happening on 12 March 1823, and this one on March 8th 1880. I copy it from the Chester Chronicle for March 13:-

"Coursing at Chester.- on Monday morning a hare was seen in Lower Bridge Street, Chester making its way towards the Cross. a labouring man living in the neighbourhood, who has a grey-hound, or a dog of that class, slipped the animal at the hare. An exiting chase ensued. On reaching the cross the hare turned down Watergate Street, at the bottom of which it swerved to the right along the City Wall, and a kill was finally effected close to the site of the old City Gaol."

Ledsham.
R. M.

A JOURNEY WITH CONVICTS FROM CHESTER GAOL

Thinking it may interest the readers of the Cheshire Sheaf, I copy this somewhat peculiar reminiscence of the good old coaching days gone by, from Reynardson's Down The Road.

"It was not very often that one met with disagreeable company outside a coach, from the fact that Coaches did not usually carry the 'hoi polloi' and the class of roughs that sometimes are to be seen in these railroad days in a third-class carriage, or in an excursion train. The class of people that are now to be seen, making excursions everywhere, from the Land's End to Johnny Groat's house, - in the good old time when 'the only steam came from the kettle' stayed at home. They attended to their business, looked after their wives and families, and were less inclined to roam than in these go-a-head days for the simple reason that they could not 'ride,' and therefore, if they wanted to go any distance, they had to walk, or go by the stage-wagon or carrier's cart, both of which were not only somewhat dearer than walking, but quite as slow. There were, however, at times a certain class of gentlemen who travelled at His Majesty's expense, and went under the denomination of 'gaol birds.' Having once had the pleasure of enjoying, their agreeable society on a coach, some notice of what took place upon this agreeable Occasion may not be an uninteresting incident of *Down the Road*.' I never heard of any other person who had the good fortune to travel with such a thorough set of scoundrels. In fact, on that memorable day, my companions were none other than The Chester Gaol Delivery!

In or about the month of November, 1834, I got upon the 'Albion' coach, which ran from Birkenhead, via Chester, to London, at Whitchurch in Shropshire. There was room on the box, so up I got by the side of the coachman. I did not at that moment take much notice of the passengers; but I recollect, that this day was cold, and they looked a 'roughish lot.' I remember that I wondered why there was room on the box, which was a very unusual thing; for the box is, and was, and I suppose always will he, the seat par excellence of all seats on a coach.

"I suppose you know what kind of a load we've got, sir?" said the coachman.

"No," I said; "they look a queer lot- what are they"

"Why," said he, "they're all gaol birds."

"Where are they going?" said I.

"Why, to Botany Bay !" said he, "and I wish they were there now, for they are inclined to give a little trouble, and would do if they had not 'ruffles' on , but they're pretty safe: they are all fast to the rail," meaning the rail that went across the coach behind the seat on the roof to prevent the luggage slipping forward. They had two keepers, or turnkeys, with them, and there was no one else on the coach but these worthies, their attendants, and myself, and the coachman and guard of the coach.

As it was known all along the road that the Chester Gaol had been 'delivered,' and that her children were going to pass that day on their way to the hulks, many 'birds of the same feather' were in waiting at the different places where we changed, to say good-bye to their old 'pals': and it was with some difficulty that the keepers could prevent their old acquaintances from plying them with drink, and giving them a parting drop to keep their spirits up. Some of them looked cold enough, for it was a real November day, and I remarked that they had not much in the shape of great coats and such little comforts In spite of all the precautions taken, some of them had had quite enough, and indeed too much, to drink, and they were somewhat inclined to be 'uproarious.' It was a comfort to us that they were handcuffed and unable to do much mischief, for which they seemed quite ready. I got off the coach at either Shiffnall or Wolverhampton, I forget now which place it was, but I remember it was beginning to be a little dusk, and we lit the lamps. The coachman called my attention to two respectable looking men, I may say they appeared to be gentlemen, who were getting out of the coach, preceded by a keeper,

"There's two of the same kind!" said he, "they've been convicted of forgery, and are going to be transported for life."

It was easy to see, as they got out of the coach, that they were handcuffed, for they were obliged to step out very 'daintily,' their hands being closely locked together in an 'iron embrace.' Being the greatest Swells of the party, and all the places on the roof being occupied by the other ruffians, they had been allowed what was called to 'ride inside' with one of the turnkeys. I was delighted not to be going any further, and was glad to see the Coachman get on his box again and drive off with his Precious load. More than one of them was half drunk, and they left, singing, "We're off to Botany Bay!" at the top of their voices. It was, as it happened, a lucky thing for me that I got off when I did for before reaching Walsall the horses shied at some sparks dying across the road from a blacksmith's shop, bolted, and, running against a lamp-post, upset the coach in the streets of Walsall. No one was killed; but the coachman never got over the injuries he received, and, I heard, ultimately died of them.

During the confusion caused by this accident, and whilst another coach and coachman were being got ready to take them in, some of the convicts contrived to get files and other implements from their friends, and in a most artistic way got their handcuffs into such a form, that they could get them off when they chose! They had made an agreement that at a certain spot they should set themselves free, and spring upon the keepers. This they did in a long, straight bit of road not far from Dunchurch. They overpowered the keepers, took their spare hand-cuffs, which they put on them, and paid the same delicate attention to the coachman and guard! They then cut the traces and let loose the horses, themselves making the best of their way across the fields. The greater part of them were retaken, but the two gentlemen forgers escaped!"

Any further information on this local incident, which must be within the recollection of some of our readers, would doubtless be interesting.
Cambridge.
T. CANN HUGHES

The Custom House

A DUEL AT BACKFORD
In the days, now fortunately historic, when the demands of injured honour could only be assuaged by an inch of steel or a bullet of lead, hostile meetings were not infrequent among the aristocracy, whether of Chester or elsewhere. I copy the following scrap from the Chester Courant *of January 30 1838;-*

"Affair of Honour.- A meeting took place at Backford, near this city, on Wednesday last, in consequence of a political misunderstanding, between Mr. William Browne, MP for Mayo, and Mr. James A. Browne, of Browne Hall, in the same county - the former attended by Mr. Somers MP for Sligo, the latter by Mr. Fitzmaurice, of Lagaturn, in the county of Mayo. On the second exchange of shots, Mr. Jas. A. Browne's ball passing through his antagonists thigh, the matter was amicably arranged. We are happy to say that the wound is not dangerous, although it may confine Mr. Browne for some time.

"We understand," adds the *Chester Chronicle,* "that the Chester police were apprised from an unknown quarter of the intended meeting, and were on the look out. Their laudable anxiety to prevent bloodshed produced a rather ludicrous result, as on the previous evening they arrested two very respectable looking gents; who, however, instead of being on such a deadly mission as the duello, were the messengers of peace, alias clergymen! Of course when the mistake was discovered they were liberated."

I find no further trace of the wounded combatant, but we may hope that he recovered from the scratch, and became a wiser and less irritable man after his experience under fire at Backford. His antagonist I find married two years afterwards, and it is to be hoped parted with his unfortunate pistols at or about that happy date.
T. HUGHES

LAWLESS CHESHIRE

A correspondent of the Oswestry Bye-gones, column of March 26, in giving some instances of 'Thieves' houses' in Wales, says:-

"Early in 1839, a *Blue Book* was published, containing a Report of the Commissioners for enquiring into the best means of establishing a Constabulary Force through England and Wales. Some of the stories told of the ways of thieves told in this report are curious and interesting. the commissioners ascertained that something like 3,000 'travellers' (i.e. thieves) made provincial tours, either at stated seasons, or when London was to hot for them; and that all over the country there were 'lodging houses for travellers,' in every town, and almost every village. These 'thieving hotels' were the flash houses of the rural district,- the receiving houses for stolen goods. The city of Chester, alone, was stated to have 150 or 200 of them and the county was generally stated to be (with Cornwall) the very worst in the Kingdom for 'Wreckers'; and it was stated that on the Cheshire coast, not far from Liverpool, "They will rob those who have escaped the perils of the sea, and come safe on shore: they will mutilate dead bodies for the sake of rings and personal ornaments."
Croeswylan, Oswestry.
A. R.

CHESTER DESCRIBED BY A TOURIST

In a small volume entitled The Ten Day's Tourist; or Sniffs of The Mountain Breeze *by William Bigg, of Luton, Bedfordshire; London: A. W. Bennet, 1865, - is the following original and pleasant description of Chester. The book referred to is a small one, and, I fancy, very little known to local collectors:-*

"This, perhaps most ancient city in the Kingdom, is in some of its features quite unique. The old wall of defence remains nearly perfect; and a pleasant walk of two or three yards wide on the top of it leads from the centre of one of the principle streets round among housetops, through gardens and orchards, whose pear trees throw up their fruit-laden branches to a level with the parapet: along the precipitous bank of the river [canal] moat, past an ancient look-out tower, now used as an observatory, at a point commanding a wide view of town and country; and along by a fragment of an ancient fortification, converted into a museum of a scientific institute; till at length that beautiful amphitheatre of the Roodeye, the Chester racecourse, stretches into view, its magic circle bounded by a grand stand of nature's own making. Beyond this there is the single-span stone bridge over the river Dee, a marvel of elegance, expansion, and symmetry. The special peculiarity of Chester is, however, the 'Row'. In the ancient streets intersecting at the heart of the city, the foot-way for passengers runs

The Water Tower

through what was originally the ground floor of the houses on each side of the road, the basement storey now fronting on to the carriage way beneath. The shops under this singular arrangement, are set back into what, under ordinary circumstances would have been the back parlour of the establishment; and the public walk under the ceiling of the floor of the drawing-room or best sleeping chamber above. Once landed in one of these Rows, the fair sex may do their shopping without parasol or umbrella , having a good house over-head, and at the same time an open look out over the public street, and an unrestricted circulation of fresh air. There are about Chester many old houses worth looking at for their quaint exterior, and curious history. The fish and vegetable market, as in every strange town, is also worth a peep. In the streets the Welsh costume of many of the country people reminds you that you are still in the near neighbourhood of Cambria; from whose lakes and mountains you will return with, I doubt not, fresh braced nerves and energies renewed to your professional engagements, prepared to fight with greater vigour and brighter cheerfulness the great battle of life."

There is a freshness and novelty about this chatty description of our old-world city that powerfully attracted my notice as I read it the other day for the first time at the Capel Curig Hotel; so much that I determined to copy it out in order to its insertion and preservation in The Sheaf.
G. T.

FENIAN RAID ON CHESTER

Eleven years have elapsed since this adroightly planned but fortunately discovered, plot to seize the ancient city and castle broke like a thunderbolt upon us all. The incident, startling as it was at the time, has passed into the domain of history now; a suggestion or two, then, in reference to it may not be out of place in the Cheshire Sheaf. *It seems to me that nothing for a century or two has occurred at Chester so fraught with serious*

consequences to the city and country as that treasonable attempt must have proved, and had not the conspirators antidote - the informer - enabled the arm of authority to counteract it. Surely, then, now that the aroused passions and prejudices on both sides thereon have, as we may hope, entirely subsided; and now that we are able to review the whole facts, free from the frenzy and exaggeration (and, I might add, the senseless ridicule and unbelief) of the immediate day, it will be worth the while of some efficient pen aquainted personally with all the circumstances, to write the history of that, thank God, futile attempt on the sacredness of law and order. The whole thing is possible now; twenty years hence the men best qualified by personal knowledge and official position to undertake the duty will likely enough have all passed away. I have one in my mind's eye now, who was then, as he is still, an energetic servant of the city, and who must almost of necessity have at his command information that has never perhaps to this hour been made fully known.
G. T.

CHESHIRE CHEESE CUSTOMS

I think the following Note, which I found in the Manchester City News *for February, is deserving permanent record in the county to which it belongs. I therefore send it under the hope you may give it a home in* The Sheaf:-

"Cheshire has long been famous for its cheese, and some old Cheshire farmers are very proud, and justly so, of the produce of their dairies. In connection with selling and weighing cheese some very curious customs and prejudices have grown up, and, as I have never seen any account of them in print, I think they may be worth recording.

The price at which a farmer sold his cheese was always considered a profound secret, and was rarely told to any one, not always even to his own wife. The reason for this rcticence will be pretty plain when we remember that, in Cheshire. the dairy was entirely under the management of the farmer's wife and daughters: and as every farmer in the county believed that the best cheese in the county was made by his own wife, none of them would tell the price at which they had sold their cheese, for fear of destroying this dearly cherished illusion.

It used to be a standing rule with a good many old farmers to insist on cash payment in gold, as soon as the cheese had been weighed. The reason they gave was, that they liked the cheese and the money to sleep together one night. All the cheese made before the cows were turned to grass, which always took place on Old May-day, or earlier if there was any grass for them to eat, was called 'boose cheese.' This was sold to the dealer (who by the way was always called a factor), as soon as ready usually from June to September. About the month of October the farmer usually sold his first hundred cheeses, that is, one hundred cheeses reckoned forward from the day on which he turned his cows out to grass. This was to him the great event of the year.

After he had agreed with the factor about the price there was another difficulty to be got over. The cheese must be weighed, but how ? The farmer had no means of weighing 100 or even 50 cheeses at once; and as he frequently could not read or write a statement of the weights of 100 cheeses, to be added up when all had been weighed, was quite out of the question. The farmer, however, had a very primitive way of getting over this difficulty. He had got an ordinary pair of scales and two 60lb. weights, which added together, were equal to 120lbs., or one long cwt. He ascertained how many cheeses came nearest to that weight, and then got a quantity of boulder stones of various sizes, which he used instead of small weights, and when he had weighed the first lot he found the weight to be one cwt. and say four boulder stones. These stones were then placed on the floor near to the end of the scales on which the cheese had been placed, and were then called cheese. The fact that a cwt. of cheese had been weighed was then recorded on the wall of the cheese room.

This was usually done by a scratch made with a rusty nail. The process was then repeated, and some more stones added to or deducted from the pile: or possibly a corresponding pile of stones begun at the other end of the scales, and if so, these were called weights. When all the cheese had been weighed, and the number of cwts. ascertained by counting the marks on the wall, the two piles of stones, or cheese and weights, as they were called, were balanced, the one against the other, and the surplus or deficiency was added to, or deducted from, the total quantity as the case might be.

This custom, though now obsolete, was quite common in Cheshire in the early part of the present century. Education has taught the farmer how to weigh his cheese, but somehow too frequently he finds that his wife has forgotten how to make it.

Cheshire cheese is always sold by the farmer to the dealer by the cwt. of 120 lbs. Prejudice and an aversion to change have doubtless had much to do with the retention of this old system; but the facilities which it afforded for making easy calculations have, probably, had more to do with its continuance to the present time. That it is much simpler to use the long than the short cwt. will, I think, be clearly seen from the following figures:-

SHORT WEIGHT:

1lb. cheese,	@8d.=0s.8d.
1cwt (112lbs)	@8d.=74s.8d.
1 ton	@8d.=£74.13s.8d.

LONG WEIGHT:

1 lb.	@8d.=0s.8d.
1cwt (120lbs)	@8d.=80s.8d.
1 ton	@8d.=£80.0s.8d.

Farmers have often been advised by their friends to give up this old custom, but so far, I believe, without any practical result. When the duty on foreign corn was abolished, many farmers in Cheshire came to the conclusion that they were going to be ruined and that any further effort on their part would be useless unless something was done to help them by the landowners or the Legislature, or by both combined. So a meeting was held at

Congleton and the farmers stated their case which, if I remember rightly, simply amounted to a request to have the corn duty reimposed, or their rents lowered by about fifty per cent. It is scarcely necessary to say that the latter proposal was not accepted, and a clerical landowner who was present told the farmers that it was useless to pass laws in favour of a class, who were too stupid to take advantage of laws which had already been passed for their special advantage. For instance, he said, if they would only sell their cheese by the cwt, of 112lbs. instead of 120lbs. they would by this means alone increase their incomes by more than six per cent ! Somehow the farmers did not seem to see it.

Wythenshawe
THOMAS WORTHINGTON"
Northendon
E. L. Y. DEACLE

CHESTER COFFEE TAVERNS

I question if there be, in any city town in England, two more picturesque examples of a now popular and philanthropic movement, than the two Coffee Houses recently established under such flattering auspices at Chester. They were both of them formerly well-known hostelries, and good specimens of the old fashioned wood and plaster gauged structures, for which the County of Chester has always been celebrated. The 'Little Nags Head'- the one first converted to temperance principles,- was entrusted by the Duke of Westminster, its owner, to the restoring hand of Mr. John Douglas, of Chester, who has reproduced a really beautiful facade, deservedly admired by all who pretend to the smallest architectural taste. The second Coffee Tavern, formerly the 'Falcon Inn' is in Lower Bridge Street; and, beyond a few internal alterations to adapt it to its present purpose, remains almost in its original state,- a picturesque feature of a picturesque locality.

And now for my Query. When and where was the first Coffee Tavern set up at Chester,- prior I mean, to those modest efforts quietly put forth when the Temperance Movement took first public root in England say half a century ago?
A . WOODMAN

The Falcon Tavern

Photographs:

Frontispiece
The Old Dee Bridge: Built in the late 14th century on the site of an earlier Roman bridge and the original ferry crossing to Handbridge, it was widened in 1826.

The Grosvenor Bridge: Designed by the great Victorian architect, Thomas Harrison, who had been commissioned by the Earl of Grosvenor, the bridge was built between 1827-1832 and opened by Princess Victoria.

The Anchorite's Cell: References to an anchorite cell attached to St. John's Church date from the 11th century. A Saxon church, which is part of the legend of King Edgar and his royal oarsmen in the 9th century, served as the first Cathedral when the diocese was located in Chester: a role later fulfilled by St. John's. The first record of anchorites in this building dates from the 14th century.

Godstall Lane: Which connects Chester Cathedral with the Eastgate Rows follows a Roman pathway.

The Wolfgate: Originally called 'Wolfeld's Gate', it dates from Aethelflaed's extension of the Roman walls in 907. It was rebuilt in the late 17th century, making it the oldest surviving gate in the city.

The Cloisters: The cloisters as they now stand in Chester Cathedral were rebuilt in the 15th century and altered again in the 19th to enclose them. Their location to the North of the Abbey Church is unusual in a monastic establishment: cloisters were usually built to the South of the Church, but because Chester was an established town before the Abbey was built, they were sited to the North.

The Blue Bell: Still a successful Chester restaurant, the Blue Bell was built in 1494 and first licensed as an inn in 1540.

King Charles' Tower: Also known as the Phoenix Tower, formed part of the original Roman walls. Traditionally, it is the place from which Charles I is said to have watched the Battle of Rowton Moor in 1645. It was rebuilt in the 18th century.

Whitefriars Street: The original street line of Whitefriars is Roman. The street is named for the Carmelite Friary established there in 1277. The house was built in 1658.

Chester Cathedral: The Benedictine Abbey of St. Werburgh was founded by Hugh Lupus, the 2nd Earl of Chester in 1092, on the site of a Saxon church rededicated to St. Werburgh in 907. In 1541, after the dissolution of the monasteries, the Abbey became Chester Cathedral. As with all mediaeval buildings, the Cathedral has been built and rebuilt on numerous occasions. Much of the modern facade dates from a major 19th century restoration by Sir George Gilbert Scott, although work continues to the present day.

The Consistory Court: Built between 1490 and 1530, the Consistory Court was one of two courts within the precincts of the Abbey, later the Cathedral: the Consistory Court tried crimes in Canon Law and was attached to the Archdiocese; St. Thomas' Court, held in the Refectory, was in effect the Church's civil law court.

The Bridge of Sighs: In 1793, this pedestrian bridge was built to connect Chester Gaol with the Bluecoat School in order to allow condemned prisoners access to the Chapel.

Watergate Street and Watergate Rows: These houses are typical of many in Watergate Street, including God's Providence House. The Rows had been considered a Victorian fake, but recent restoration work has given ample evidence of their Tudor provenance. The house to the right was the scene of the Chester Puppet Show Tragedy in 1772, which would account for its substantial reconstruction. The crypts below both houses are mediaeval.

Chester Castle: The original castle was built in 1070 and rebuilt in stone in the 12th century. It has been altered substantially since.

The Footbridge: A footbridge connecting the city to the new suburb of Queen's Park was first built in 1852, it was rebuilt in 1923.

The Town Hall: Chester's great monument to Victorian prosperity was designed by Thomas Harrison and opened by the Prince of Wales in 1869. The sculpture which was erected in the Town Hall Square in 1992 is by Stephen Broadbent, it is a Celebration of Chester, depicting Thanksgiving, Protection and Industry.

The Oak Coffin at St. John's Church: The original church was built in 1075, the Eastern chapels of which these are the ruins date from the 13th and 14th centuries. The oak coffin was disinterred in the churchyard early in the 19th century and placed in a niche in the walls.

The Custom House: Adjacent to Trinity Church, now the Guild Hall, the Custom House was built in 1868.

The Water Tower: Also known as the New Tower, it was constructed in 1323, to extend the city's fortifications to the water's edge. It is connected to Bonewaldesthorne's Tower on the North West angle of the walls. It was used as a museum by the Mechanics Institute between 1838 and 1885.

The Falcon Tavern: Built in 1626, incorporating a 13th century cellar, it was the Grosvenor family's town house. It has undergone an award winning restoration.